Handbuildi

HANDBUILDING

Michael Hardy

A & C Black · London

University of Pennsylvania Press · Philadelphia

First published in Great Britain 2000
A & C Black (Publishers) Limited
35 Bedford Row
London WC1R 4JH

ISBN 0-7136-4841-4

Published simultaneously in the USA by
University of Pennsylvania Press
4200 Pine Street
Philadelphia, PA 19104-4011

ISBN 0-8122-1755-1

Cover illustration
Bottles by Michael Hardy

Back illustration
Loose Lips Sink Ships, 1997, by Neil Brownsword

Frontispiece
Coiled pot by Monica Young

Design and typesetting by Alan Hamp
Printed and bound in Malaysia by
Times Offset (M) Sdn. Bhd.

Contents

Acknowledgements

I would like to express my gratitude and thanks to all of those who have helped in the preparation of this book.

First of all I would like to thank all the potters who so generously gave their time to talk to me and provide information about their work, for allowing me to see their studios and for making available photographs of their ceramics: Paul Astbury, Ian Auld, Gordon Baldwin, John Berry, Betty Blandino, Alison Britton, Neil Brownsword, Delan Cookson, Philippa Cronin, Jill Crowley, Elizabeth Fritsch, Carol Greenaway, Regina Heinz, Ewen Henderson, Wendy Hoare, Mo Jupp, Christy Keeney, Gabriele Koch, Peter Lane, Gillian Lowndes, Kate Malone, Ursula Morley-Price, Sara Radstone, David Roberts, Martin Smith and Monica Young.

Thanks also to my wife Dawn and to Valerie Robinson and Brian Lubrani for their help, encouragement and support. I would also like to add my appreciation of Linda Lambert for her patience and practical advice, and to Dawn Hardy and Valerie Robinson for their work in producing the sequence photographs.

Thanks to the following museums and institutions for permission to reproduce photographs of ceramics in their collections:

Buckinghamshire County Museum
The British Museum
The Crafts Council
University of Cambridge Museum of Archaeology and Anthropology

and to Potterycrafts Ltd for providing photographs of their equipment.

Introduction

Once primitive man had discovered that a certain kind of mud could be moulded and shaped, the long process of developing ways of manipulating this material, called clay, and refining techniques, began and continues to the present day.

If we watch the instinctive reactions of young children when they first handle clay it gives us some insight into how early man might have responded to this plastic material. There is an instinctive desire to squeeze and press the soft clay into a shape and to pinch and pull out extensions to model it into a form. A rotary movement with a piece of clay between the hands, or on a flat surface with one hand, soon results in a ball shape. It is not long before a finger is pushed into the ball of clay to produce a hollow in the centre. Similarly a back and forth movement with clay, between the hands or on a surface, produces a rope or coil of clay. The potential is soon seen for building up the coils one upon another and joining them together to form the wall of a hollow vessel. Another reaction is to flatten it by pressing or beating until it becomes a slab or sheet of clay. All are examples of the instinctive beginnings of the traditional handbuilding processes and techniques.

The discovery that fire hardened the clay artefacts and made them more durable, accelerated the desire to become more skillful, as the potential of clay to make containers that could be used for cooking, storing and drinking increased the importance of pottery making. These skills were developed and passed on from one generation to the next.

The versatility of clay was also recognised. The fact that it could be used in certain ways when it was soft and moist, and in other ways when it was plastic or leatherhard, also opened up further potential for technical development and a wider range of uses in both constructing and decorating. Clay has great creative potential but it also has limitations. It can crack, sag, collapse, stiffen and harden or just stick to the hands. As a result certain basic handbuilding techniques that will ensure greater success have evolved. These have become part of the tradition of pottery making and have been passed down through the centuries. These techniques are few in number but, unlike the throwing techniques that are used to construct the more symmetrical and restricted wheel-thrown forms, they can be developed or combined to maximise personal expression, and allow endless possibilities in the making of functional and sculptural forms.

So how do we define handbuilt ceramics? At one time that question could have been simply answered by the statement that it was 'the making of pottery without any mechanical aid'. It would have ruled out the use of the potter's wheel and any of the industrial

Head by Michael Hardy, 1997 h. 37 cm w. 26 cm
Moulded slip and fibreglass matting head on a slab-built base

casting and moulding processes. The traditional making methods of pinching, coiling and slab building would have covered the handbuilding processes, with the possible inclusion of moulds for the making of pressed dishes.

In the last 25 years, boundaries between the making methods have become increasingly blurred, and potters have freely combined traditional handbuilding techniques. It is also not unusual for potters to take thrown forms and to use them as a basis or an extension for their handbuilding. The industrial casting and moulding processes are no longer seen as just a sterile means of repetition, but as a means of producing forms that can be developed, or added to, by handbuilding.

One of the most interesting developments in recent years has been that some potters no longer just accept the work as finished when it comes out of the glaze firing. They often wish to continue working on the ceramic form. This might be just a matter of further painting and refiring, or it could involve the addition of non-ceramic materials to create a mixed-media ceramic form. It is also possible to change and further develop the surface of the fired ceramic by sandblasting, grinding and polishing.

I have found that most handbuilders still work with the clay in an expressive and direct way, exploiting the plastic qualities of the material, but boundaries are being moved, new technologies are being explored and definitions are changing.

I have tried to reflect these changes in this book and have included potters who are working on the edge of the field of handbuilding, but who might not be considered handbuilders in the traditional sense. I have also included some techniques that are not usually included in books on handbuilding.

I also want to share my personal experience of making handbuilt ceramics, lecturing on the subject and of teaching students for many years. I hope that the book will be a springboard for those who need step-by-step instruction to learn a specific handbuilding technique, and that it will also be a means of exploring techniques to enhance imaginative and creative development, and thereby meet the expressive needs of the more experienced student or potter. This book will focus upon handbuilding and will only touch incidentally upon decorating, glazing and firing, when talking about specific works.

The photographs of both traditional and contemporary handbuilt forms show not only how potters continue to shape clay by hand, but how, in doing so, they can produce something beyond the utilitarian. I hope that the photographs will inspire the reader to look at other works by these ceramic artists and the many others impossible to include in a publication of this size. In the preparation of this book I have spent many fascinating hours in museums and had the pleasure of visiting and talking to many of the leading contemporary makers of handbuilt ceramics. They have generously discussed their ideas and sources of inspiration and readily shared their techniques and ways of working. They have also made available photographs of their work to illustrate the variety and richness of the handbuilt methods of working with clay.

Finally, it is important to remember that techniques are not an end in themselves, but a means through which artists can express their ideas in clay.

Vounos Tomb Vessel from Cyprus
Courtesy of the University of Cambridge Museum of Archaeology & Anthropology

Chapter One
A Brief Historical Background of Handbuilt Ceramics

The use of clay seems to have been developed independently by people in different parts of the world. The earliest uses were probably for strengthening buildings and shelters, or for body identification marks. Because of its fragility, nomadic people would have had little use for pottery, but they did use clay to model the miniature sculptures which have been found in many parts of the world, including Mesopotamia and the Indus valley. These sculptures were often in the form of small ritual figures related to fertility or hunting.

The making of pottery really began when tribes ceased to be nomadic and formed settled communities. The discovery that the red heat of a fire (600°C/1112°F) transformed clay into a more permanent material called pottery probably happened gradually and in many parts of the world at the same time. There are various theories, one being that the clay lining the firepit was found to have hardened and changed, or another, often quoted, that the clay smeared on the inside of baskets dried away as a clay shell, or that the baskets were burned away, probably by accident at first, to leave a pottery shell. This discovery produced artefacts that have told us so much about our past; although easily broken, the shards or remains have not decayed or decomposed, but have been recovered, often with the remains of their contents, to tell us something of the life of their

makers and how the vessels themselves were made. Some of the best examples have been found in burial sites, where they have been used as funerary urns. The earliest pottery found dates from about 7000 BC, but some of the most interesting examples have come from the Neolithic and Bronze Age periods 3000–1000 BC. Most of these examples, with the exception of modelled and slab-built troughs, are round, despite not having being made on a pottery wheel. The roundness comes naturally from the need to turn the pots, or to walk around larger pots, as they are handbuilt. The early potters often sat on the ground with the pot resting on a disc or mat on the ground in front of them, using their legs to support the pot as it was made. These methods enabled the pot to be turned as the potter worked.

The earliest pots made in Britain dating from about 2000 BC were handbuilt forms, often with distinctive collars or rims of clay, and have mostly been recovered from burial sites. They clearly had a ritual use, but were also used for general domestic purposes, especially for the storage of food.

It is impossible to say with any certainty when and where the potter's wheel first came into use, as it was probably developed by several civilisations in different countries at about the same time. The potter's wheel was to dominate the making of pottery until well into the 20th century, and as a result of this technique, forms became more standardised. All the pots made on the wheel had to be round, without angles or sharp curves, unless altered after throwing. Although the use of the potter's wheel was dominant, handbuilding still survived, as in some areas the use of traditional techniques was too well established to be easily abandoned, even if the pottery wheel was available. Often, because the local clay was coarse and unsuitable for throwing, it could be shaped more readily by hand and would withstand the rapid drying and firing processes. In some places handbuilding was continued as a means of producing larger forms. Some of the best examples of handbuilt pottery have been discovered in Africa and Central America. In these cultures the making of pottery is completely interwoven with the social fabric and daily life. Quite often it is the women who make the pots in between their other chores, while the men dig the clay and fire the pots, or in some societies are responsible for the decoration. The division of labour varies from one culture to another. One thing that is common to much of the ethnic work is its spontaneity and vigour. This has been much admired by the handbuilders working in the second half of the 20th century.

In the first half of the 20th century, pottery making was largely dominated by the throwing and moulding processes, mainly in factory production.

Below
Alwinton Food Vessel (Bronze Age)
Courtesy of the British Museum

Right
Water Pot from Africa, Nigeria, Ibo
Courtesy of the British Museum

As the studio movement grew in Britain, it was dominated by Bernard Leach, who was to promote the combining of art with utility in the oriental style.

Even after the Second World War British studio ceramics was dominated by the production of thrown ware, narrowly focused on the oriental style. It was the influence of Lucie Rie and Hans Coper, and the teaching in certain art schools, that began to challenge the dominance of the Leach philosophy and create a situation wherein handbuilding became more acceptable. In the 1960s the influences and sources of contemporary art began to have an affect, and many potters began to see themselves as artists who happened to work with clay. The boundary between art and craft was becoming more and more blurred, and the boundary between the vessel and sculpture less clear.

A new modernism in the field of ceramics began with the handbuilders of the 1960s. The term 'pottery' was often abandoned for the term 'ceramics', which seemed more appropriate to cover a spectrum of work now wider than throwing and functionalism. The techniques of handbuilding opened up a wide range of possibilities for anyone working with clay, especially for some of those potters who had originally trained as painters or sculptors and did not feel the need to use materials in the same way the traditional craftsmen potters of the past had done. There was also a strong influence from the USA, where a more liberal and expressive approach was already evident, especially in the work and teaching of Peter Voulkos.

Awareness of other artists such as Picasso and Miró, who were using clay in new and exciting ways, added impetus to this modern movement in ceramics. A new type of handbuilt form began to appear, at first mainly in the form of pots made with coarse grogged clays and having an earthy and robust character, with surfaces that were textured and stonelike in appearance. In the 1970s there was a strong movement away from this approach and more white clays and porcelains were used. Delicate pinched forms proliferated and casting techniques were used to produce precisely made shapes. The boundaries between industrial processes and the studio approach were also beginning to break down.

Throwing had given the potter great speed of production, necessary in the making of functional ware, but handbuilding was giving the potter greater freedom of form. The new generation of potters began to see themselves as artists in clay and to seek new ideas, inspiration and stimuli, but they had to match these with the techniques that were needed to translate the concept into a concrete form or object. Traditional handbuilding techniques were constantly being developed to meet the expressive needs of individual potters and when limitations were encountered, new ways of working with clay were found. These often involved the combining of techniques or even the use of other materials to give strength or support. Some pieces had to be fired several times, or have clay or non-ceramic additions incorporated after firing.

Chapter Two
Clay

Clay is usually accepted as a wonderful plastic material that responds directly and immediately to our fingers. We can squeeze and press it into practically any shape and it will retain that shape. The potter, however, needs to have a greater knowledge of the varieties and working qualities of clays in order to ensure that they are suitable for the techniques being used and that the forms he or she creates will survive the drying and firing stages of the process.

The formation of clay

Clay is an abundant material covering much of the world's surface. It is continuously being formed by the decomposition of igneous rocks, the result of glacial action and weathering processes. These processes also determine the plasticity and colour of the clay. If the clay remains on the site where it was formed it is known as residual or primary clay. The best known of these is China clay or kaolin. They are usually the purest and whitest of the clays, but are usually less plastic because they have a large particle size.

The particle size is an important factor in determining the plasticity of the clay. If the clay has been carried from its site of formation by water, wind or glacier and deposited in new beds, it is known as secondary or sedimentary clay. While being transported, these clays deposit many of the larger particles and as a result the secondary or sedimentary clays have a smaller particle size which makes them more plastic and increases their workability. They also pick up impurities on route, which often affects their colour and can make them only suitable for firing at lower temperatures. These clays are often grey-yellow or red-brown in colour and include the ball clays.

The structure of clay

Chemically, clay consists of alumina, silica and water, and its chemical formula is $Al_2O_3 - 2SiO_2 - 6H_2O$. The simplest way to understand the structure of clay is to remember that the particles of clay are flat and plate-like. Its versatility and many forms come from the fact that when wet they slide and cling together, when dry they lock together in a solid mass and when too much water is present they float apart in a sticky slurry or become a slip. By subjecting clay to high firing temperatures the potter turns it back to a rock-like state.

Clay bodies

To make them more suitable for the potter to use, different clays can be blended and other ingredients added. This is known as a clay 'body' and can either be mixed by the potter or, more usually, bought from a supplier, who either makes a standard range of clay bodies or can make up specific mixes to meet a potter's needs. This is usually only possible if larger quantities are required. Most potters start with a standard body and then make their own adjustments. The usual method is to mix two or more clays together to change the colour slightly or to make it more suitable for whatever technique and firing temperature is going to be used.

Changing the stucture of the clay

Additions can be made to adjust the texture and mechanical strength of the clay body. Grog, which is crushed biscuit-fired clay, can be mixed into the body to give added texture and strength. It can be purchased in different degrees of fineness from almost dust to coarser grades; because it has already been fired it stiffens the clay and makes it stronger. It also makes it more open in texture and therefore reduces the risk of cracking if the clay is thick. Brick dust is another form of grog, often introduced to give added colour. Sand can be used in a similar way and can also sometimes add colour as well as texture.

Other materials such as sawdust and paper pulp are often added. These will burn away in the firing, leaving a more open and textured body that will be lighter in weight because of the more open porous ceramic which remains.

The best way to combine or mix smaller batches of clay is to slice the two or more types being mixed and to alternate the layers in a sandwich, and knead and wedge them together until they are thoroughly mixed. It may be necessary to keep cutting, sandwiching and wedging until a homogenous mass is achieved. A similar method can be used to add granular materials such as sand, grog, sawdust etc. If larger batches of any particular blend or mixture are required it would be better to use a mechanical clay mixer or pugmill.

Paper clay is usually prepared by mixing the paper pulp with clay slip in proportions of up to 50% of paper pulp. The paper slip mixture is poured onto a porous surface to remove the excess water, until it is in a workable plastic state. Paper pulp can either be purchased ready for use from a supplier or can be homemade by shredding and soaking suitable soft, uncoated paper.

Preparing the clay for use

The clay will need to be prepared for use by wedging or kneading to thoroughly mix it and to remove air bubbles that might expand and cause the clay to shatter in the firing.

Wedging is the most common method of clay preparation. Small pieces of clay can be hand wedged by tearing the pieces apart and banging them together in the hands to mix and exclude the air. Larger pieces of soft clay are cut in half with a cutting wire and then banged together on the bench, bringing the outside of one piece together with the inside of the other half. This is repeated until the lump of clay is of even consistency and no air pockets are revealed when the clay is cut.

Kneading is very difficult to describe in words, but it involves a rhythmic movement that continually rolls and turns the clay on the bench, pulling the inside clay to the outside and bursting the air bubbles as the clay is compressed. There are two main handgrips used in kneading. One usually known as the 'ox-head' or 'ram's head' involves the hands being placed at each end of a short log of clay and repeatedly slicing down with the wrists and palms as the clay is pulled forward. This movement forms an ox-head shape as the clay is worked. The other method is the 'spiral' method of kneading that involves a rhythmic push, lift and twist action with one hand below the clay and the other pushing down in a rotating movement that keeps the clay in a spiral cone shape.

If the clay is too wet or too stiff it is possible to change the consistency at this stage. If too wet, wedging the clay on a porous wooden worktop or board, or on a plaster of Paris slab, will absorb the excess moisture. It may need to be left overnight. If the clay is too stiff it helps to moisten the wedging surface with a wet sponge, thus allowing the clay to pick up moisture as it is being wedged. Water can be added to clay by making impressions or holes in the lump with a stick or rolling pin, then filling them with water which will slowly be absorbed, overnight if need be. It helps to cover the block of clay with a damp cloth to prevent the outer surface from drying in the room atmosphere.

Keeping the clay workable

It is difficult for us today to think of how clay was stored and kept in a workable state before polythene was available. I have a distant memory of rather smelly wet cloths, which had to be regularly dampened or renewed. Today the storage of clay is so much easier with plastic bins and polythene bags and sheets (assuming that everyone replaces lids and remembers to close the bag each time the clay is used). Polythene is also invaluable for keeping clay workable during the handbuilding process. It is important to know how to control the drying of the clay as you work, because

quite often it is necessary to allow the lower part of a form to stiffen in order to support the weight of the clay being added to the top. The top will, of course, need to remain soft and workable. This can often be achieved by partial covering of the form or by selective use of polythene or wet paper towels or newspaper. A hand spray that will deposit a fine mist of water on the clay surface is most useful. All this must be achieved without causing uneven drying and possible cracking. Always keep the clay waiting to be used carefully wrapped in polythene, unless you want it to be stiffening. If a piece of clay is left uncovered it is often a good idea to re-wedge it, as the outside will have dried more than the inside.

Shrinkage

The fact that clay shrinks as it dries and also when it vitrifies during the firing process is something that the handbuilder needs to be constantly thinking about. Clay shrinks first as the water in the plastic clay evaporates and the particles draw closer together. This means that the shrinkage, like the plasticity, depends on the particle size and the amount of water present in the clay. Further shrinkage takes place during vitrification, as certain components in the clay melt, altering its structure.

It is important to remember that different types of clay or clays with varying physical make-up or water content cannot be successfully joined. Clay walls of different thicknesses shrink at different rates which may cause cracking.

As forms dry and are fired, provision must be made for the movement of the clay due to shrinkage. Drying pots should not be left stuck to boards, but a sprinkling of grog or a piece of cloth or newspaper should be placed underneath to facilitate the movement. Forms that stand on more than one point should be placed on a slab of clay that will shrink with the form and not cause it to be pulled apart by the stress.

More specific references will be made to shrinkage problems in later sections.

Types of clay

Clay bodies tend to be grouped according to their colour, texture and the temperature to which they can be fired, and most suppliers' lists will give information on all of these.

Potters tend to find a clay body that is suitable for their method of working, the character of the form they wish to make and the temperature to which they wish to fire. As they become more familiar with its working properties they tend to keep to that clay body, perhaps only modifying it slightly for specific uses. Although the makers of handbuilt ceramics use a wide range of clays from earthenware red to lightly grogged buff stoneware bodies, there are some that are more used than others. These are the white stoneware bodies textured with Molochite and sold as 'T' Material and 'C' Material. Another very popular clay with handbuilders is the grogged orange/buff clay known as 'Crank'.

Reference will be made to the clays used when discussing the work of individual potters throughout the book.

Reusing clay

Any used clay that has not been fired can be recycled by just soaking it down in a bucket or bin full of water, depending on the quantity. Mechanical clay mixers and pugmills are useful ways to reconstitute clay, but if no mechanical aid is available, the methods described above can be used to dry the clay to the required consistency, after which it can be wedged in the normal way. Newly reconstituted or pugged clay is better if stored in polythene bags for a week or two to allow the added water to penetrate the structure of the clay more evenly. This will improve the workability of the clay. If used too quickly the clay can be what is known as 'short' and have a tendency to tear easily, leaving ragged edges.

Chapter Three
The Working Space, Equipment and Tools

To visit an artist's studio or craft workshop is like going behind the stage of a theatre or into the kitchen of a good restaurant. It is a way of gaining some insight into what goes on behind the scenes to create the end product. It is pleasing to note that more 'Open Studio' days are being organised to allow visitors to see where and how the work is made. To see the rows of tools and the equipment used, as well as to see work at various stages of making, all add to a greater appreciation and understanding of the artists and their work.

A selection of tools used for handbuilding

Working space

Handbuilding need not require a large working area and I have known people who have worked in their kitchens and other family rooms. Although handbuilding is not as messy as throwing, it does cause dust, so working in the home is not ideal, unless a specific part of the house can be kept as a studio – a cellar or basement is probably best. Outbuildings such as garages or sheds are also suitable, but need to be properly insulated, or the water in the clay and any wet pots will freeze in cold weather. This will cause the pots to collapse and

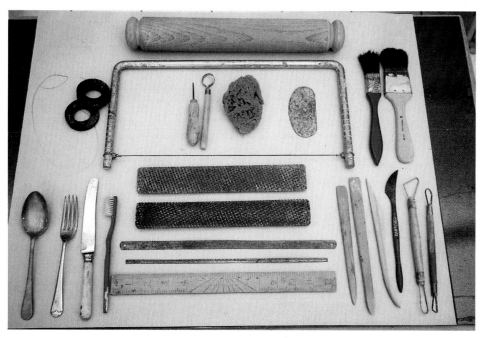

Above
Extruder used for
making clay coils
*Courtesy of
Potterycrafts Ltd*

Left
The workbench in
Jill Crowley's studio
showing a selection
of her tools

the clay to become wet and sticky on the
outside and stiff on the inside when it
thaws. It will also make working
conditions less comfortable at certain
times of the year. Although a great deal
of space is not necessary for the making
of handbuilt forms there does need to be
space and shelves for materials and
equipment. The size of the workspace for
storing work at various stages of making
and drying must also be considered.

Equipment

To start with, only very basic equipment
is necessary, such as a work surface,
table or bench, and bins or containers
for storing the used clay, preferably
plastic bins which are lighter to move
and less noisy to use. A turntable is a
useful piece of equipment, but a board
on a bowl can be a substitute. It must be
remembered that equipment for other

stages in the making process, for glazing and firing, will also be required. More specialised equipment can be purchased, such as an extruder for making coils, a slab roller and a pugmill or clay mixer, but this is not essential for the maker of handbuilt forms.

Tools

For a potter the best tools are the fingers, and many tools available are just seen as an extension of the fingers, to use or reach where fingers are too short or wrongly shaped.

The tools needed for handbuilding are really very few, especially when starting out. Although tools can be purchased from suppliers, many are to be found in the home and garage. A knife, fork and spoon make a good start to any toolbox, and old hacksaw and Surform blades are ideal for working the surface of clay.

Slab rolling machine
Courtesy of Potterycrafts Ltd

Tools are very personal to potters and many make and adapt tools or everyday objects to suit their particular needs. As the toolbox is added to, all sorts of objects that are seen to have potential for scraping, smoothing, shaping, or for making textures and patterns are included. Some techniques demand specific tools, such as rolling pins and wooden lathe strips for rolling slabs, or wooden beaters for shaping coiled pots.

I have listed below a range of useful tools according to their function, and when discussing the methods of different potters later in the book I have referred to any favourite tool or piece of equipment.

Cutting:
– length of twisted wire (brass picture wire) or nylon monofilament (fishing line) with rings or toggles on each end, for slicing clay
– knife
– wire bow or harp for cutting slabs
– needle
– multipurpose tools or coilers

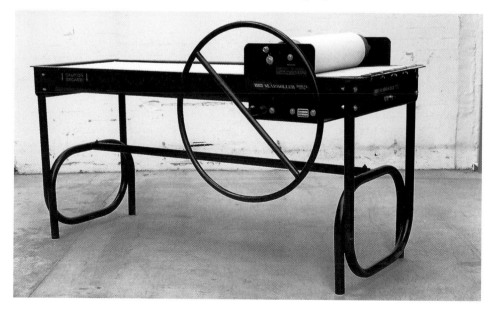

Shaping:
– wooden rolling pin
– modelling tools
– paddles or bats for beating the walls
of the pots, made from lengths of
wood or adapted from wooden spoons
or wooden toy bats
– wooden throwing ribs

Smoothing:
– rubber kidney
– table spoon
– pebbles
– sheets of plastic kitchen-pot scourer
for smoothing the dry clay

Scraping:
– hacksaw blade
– Surform blade
– steel kidney
– table fork

Keeping the clay workable:
– polythene bags and sheets
– water atomiser or spray

Cleaning up:
– paint scrapers
– brushes
– sponges

Chapter Four
Pinching

Introduction

Pinching is often thought of as a beginner's technique. I have certainly found in my teaching that because the ball of clay is usually held and worked in the hands it is a good way for a beginner to 'get the feel of the clay' and a feeling for the three-dimensional qualities of a form, but to make a good pinched pot great control and subtlety is needed. A pinched pot can be a simple bowl shape or a complex asymmetric form, and it is important to appreciate its potential for a wide range of creative expression.

Background

Pinching was probably one of the earliest methods of making a pot as it is an instinctive response to clay. The technique of pinching or squeezing the clay into a shape was used for making some of the earliest small ritualistic figurines and animal forms. The first hollow shapes were probably made by pinching and pressing the soft clay over a rounded stone or into a hollow in the ground or rock where it could be left until the clay stiffened enough for it to be removed. In primitive African communities a variation of this is often used when a larger lump of clay

is placed in the bottom of a hollow form, such as a piece of dried gourd or the lower part of a broken pot, and the clay pressed and beaten up the wall of the hollow shape. The clay is pressed between the supporting hollow form and the hand, although sometimes a pebble or wooden beater is used.

In post-war Britain **Ruth Duckworth** was one of the influential small group of potters who did so much to make handbuilding acceptable. During the 1960s she began to produce, alongside her coiled pots, many small pinched forms. These were usually in porcelain

Porcelain Form by Ruth Duckworth, 1966/67 h. 124 mm. Pinched with celadon glaze
Courtesy of Buckinghamshire County Museum

and inspired by natural forms such as shells, fungi and stones. They retained the essence of the natural forms yet became sculptural pieces in their own right. Many of the potters who use this technique have in some way been influenced by Ruth Duckworth.

Clays

The technique relies on the plastic nature of clay which stretches when squeezed between the thumb and fingers. Most clays are suitable for this method of making, but the plasticity of the clay will determine the type of form that can be made. The coarser, heavily grogged clay bodies will only be suitable for the simple, heavier and more robust shapes. To make the finer and more delicate forms a more plastic clay will be needed. The colour of the clay might be a factor to consider, and if you wish the clay to become translucent when pinched very thin, then a porcelain body must be used. The type of firing will also be a factor to consider; as already discussed not all clays will fire to stoneware temperatures. If the pots are to be raku-fired, then the coarser grogged clays are more suitable as they will withstand the thermal shock of being packed into an already heated

kiln, and being removed and cooled rapidly. The clay for pinching needs to be reasonably soft and can be prepared in the usual ways, but slapping the ball of clay firmly between the hands before starting will help to consolidate the piece and force out any remaining pockets of air. You are then ready to start making your pot.

Making a pinch pot

It is a good idea to start with a ball of clay that fits comfortably into the hand (usually about the size of a tennis ball). Then, holding the ball of clay in one hand, a hole can be pushed into the clay with the thumb of the other hand, making sure to leave enough clay for the base of the pot (usually about 1 cm or 0.5 in., although this can depend upon the character of the form you intend to make).

Slowly turning the ball of clay as you work, pinch gently with the thumb on the inside and fingers on the outside, working from the bottom – do not allow the top to open out too soon or it will have a tendency to become too wide and shallow. The thickness and evenness of the wall of the pot is ascertained purely by the fingers and the tactile experience of pinching the clay. Keep pinching and

Starting a pinched form from a ball of clay

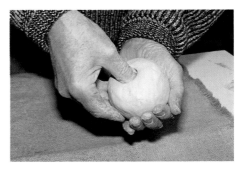

Pushing the thumb into the centre of the ball of clay

Pinching the clay between the thumb on the inside and the fingers on the outside while rotating the pot in the other hand

Thinning the wall of the pot by pinching as it is slowly turned

turning the form as you work towards the top. Control the outside and inside contours of the form by varying the pressure of the fingers and thumb; more pressure by the thumb will make the form bulge out, more by the fingers will encourage the form to close in, while an even pressure should squeeze the wall straight up.

If the clay begins to go soft and floppy then stop and leave it for a while to stiffen before continuing (it is sometimes a good idea to make several thumbpots at the same time). The pot can be rested on a dry sponge or sat in the top of a pot or any other container of a suitable size until it has stiffened. It is a good idea to drape some paper towel or tissue over the edge of the supporting container to protect the pot and to stop it sticking. If the sides are likely to collapse out then the form can be supported upside down over a suitable form like an upturned pot, but again use a paper towel to cushion the form and stop it sticking.

Alternatively, the surface of the clay may become too dry and begin to crack; this is often caused by the warmth of the fingers. Moisture needs to be restored by keeping the fingers moist and cool and

this is best done by having a wet sponge on the workbench, though some potters use saliva as a means of keeping their fingers and the surface of the clay moist and workable. Do not add water directly to the surface of the clay or it will become too wet and slippery. The rim of the pot is very important and can do much to determine the character of the form. The rim can be the same thickness as the rest of the pot or can be pinched until the clay is wafer thin. This usually results in an irregular edge which has a petal or shell like quality; it may cause the clay to split, which can look very effective and natural. If a more even or regular edge is required, the top can be trimmed or cut with a needle and smoothed using a sponge or piece of leather or polythene. A moist soft paintbrush is often useful for delicate pieces. To prevent the thin soft clay edge sticking to the fingers and possibly tearing, dust the fingertips with powdered clay.

The base of the thumbpot shaped in the hand will usually be rounded and have a natural curve; it is often a good idea to retain this rounded shape. The pot can be made to stand upright and

Pinching the edge until wafer thin

As above, side view

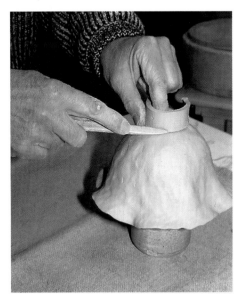

Adding a footring by cutting a strip of clay and joining it to the base of the pinched pot

become stable, either by tapping the form gently on a flat surface to give it a base or by making a slight depression in the base of the form. A larger footring can be made by joining a coil or strip of clay to the base of the pot while the form is still soft. This can be welded on with either water or slip and then the join smoothed and finished with a modelling tool.

When the form has been completed it should be dried slowly until it reaches the leatherhard stage when it can be scraped and the shape of the surface further refined using a metal kidney or piece of hacksaw blade. If it is a fine clay, a smooth polished surface can be achieved by burnishing with the back of a spoon or the bone handle of a knife. If the clay is textured with grog or sand, the texture can be exaggerated by the scraping. It sometimes helps to scrape in a direction which will enhance the contours of the form. When the pot is really dry it is possible to refine the surface further by rubbing it with a piece of plastic pot scourer or sandpaper. It is advisable to wear a mask for this.

Developing the pinching technique

Once the basic technique of pinching has been mastered, the simple bowl form can be developed. I have already described how the simple, open pinched form can have a robust, solid character or can be pinched very thin to produce fine, delicate and often fragile forms. Composite forms can be made by joining two or more pinched pots. If two thumbpots about 1 cm (0.5 in.) thick are made into simple bowl shapes with their openings about the same size, they can be firmly pressed together to make a completely spherical or egg-shaped

Joining two pinched pots

Batting the joined pebble form to change the shape

composite form. The clay must be pulled from one side of the join to the other, and smoothed to consolidate the wall of the new shape. It is important that this join is well made as in most cases it will be impossible to reach the inside of the joint.

The spherical or egg shape can then be modified and the surface compacted by gently rolling or tapping the form on a flat surface, or batting it with a flat piece of wood to make facets or more angular contours. The air trapped inside the form will cushion the shape and prevent it from collapsing if not too much force is used. When you are satisfied with the shape, it will be necessary to make an opening in the form to allow the trapped air to escape when it expands during the firing. The opening can be part of the overall form or can be concealed underneath if there is no practical or aesthetic reason for it being near the top. If the opening is large enough this might provide an opportunity to smooth the inside. It is

Three Pebble Forms by Michael Hardy

also possible to blow into the opening, like a balloon, to inflate the form, giving a greater tension to the contours.

The conglomerate form made from two thumbpots can also be developed by adding coils to the opening, to form a neck, or to extend the form to make a greater feature of the opening.

The pinching technique is also often used in combination with other techniques to bring a livelier, more organic quality, to more rigid or formal forms. The rims of thrown or coiled forms are sometimes pinched to allow a tighter or more rigid contour to interplay more freely with the surrounding space. It can be like a plant moving from a rigid and formal stem and leaves to the delicacy of the flower.

A potter who has developed, with a very personal and bold style, the technique of extending a pinched form with coils, is **Ursula Morley-Price**. She usually starts with a simple thumbpot which is then extended with coils. In the case of the 'Ruffle' pots, the form is smoothed both inside and out using metal and rubber kidneys, once the required height is reached. A larger coil is then added to the top and, when joined, lips are pulled out all round the rim using one finger to pull outwards, while two fingers of the other hand are placed either side to support the rim, as with pulling a lip on a thrown jug. Separate thin coils are then added to the projecting lips which are pinched out to exaggerate the undulating top. This is repeated until the outside ruffle is the required size. The process is then repeated on the inner rim to develop that part of the ruffle.

Her 'Flange' forms are started in the same way, but when the required height has been reached, a horizontal top is coiled on. Separate wedges of clay are made and a slit is cut at the wider end. The horizontal rim is forced into the slits as the wedges are joined all round the top. Coils are then built vertically onto the wedges and pinched to produce the flanges. The edges of the ruffles and flanges are often picked out with oxides, at the glazing stage, to give greater emphasis.

Other conglomerates involve the joining of individual pinched forms to make multiple sectioned bowls or clusters of joined pots to offer adjoining containers for a variety of purposes, such as holding plants or sweets.

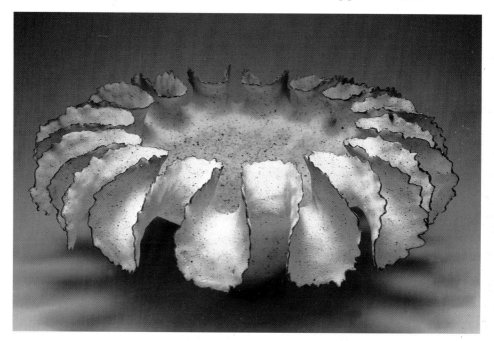

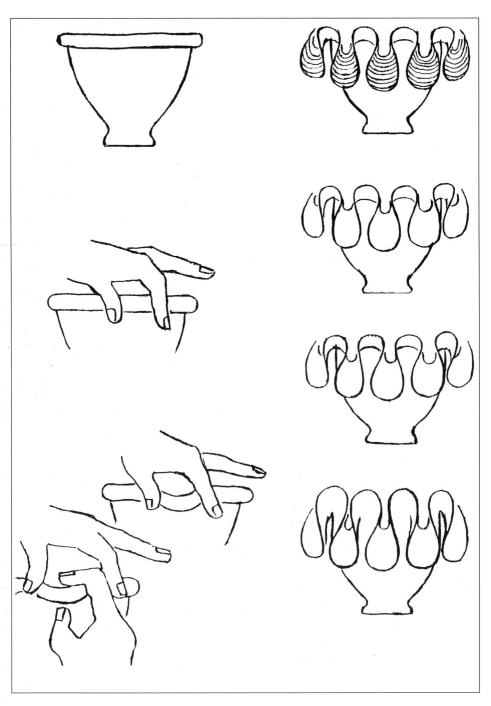

Left
Ruffle Bowl by Ursula Morley-Price

Above
Drawings by Ursula Morley-Price to show
how she handbuilds 'Ruffle' forms

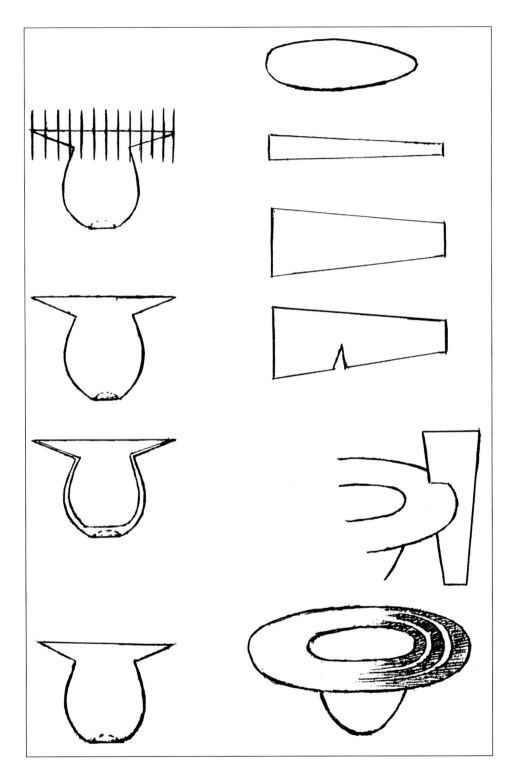

Left
Drawings by Ursula Morley-Price to show
how she constructs 'Flange' forms

Wiz Form h. 12.5 cm and Flange Form
h. 15 cm by Ursula Morley-Price
Porcelain, ash glaze

Surface treatments

There are many decorations that might
be used on pinched forms, but it is
important to remember that, because
the pots are usually small in size, the
decoration or surface treatment must
not overcrowd or detract from the
simplicity and directness of the form. It
is also important to remember that the
pot must not be made too wet when
adding slip or colour, as there is the
danger of it collapsing.

If the wall of the clay is about 1 cm
(0.5 in.) thick, it is possible to impress
shapes and patterns or textures into the
surface of the clay while it is still soft. It
is important to support the clay to
prevent splitting and distortion.
Similarly, incised or cut decorations can
be made with a variety of tools or
implements, but particularly useful are
wire loop tools or lino-cutting tools.

Porcelain

Many of the pinched forms made by
professional potters are made in
porcelain. The delicacy and thinness
that can be achieved with the pinching
technique is seen at its best with a
material such as porcelain, but I must
stress that this is not the material for the
beginner.

Porcelain is more difficult to use than
other clays because it is not as plastic; it
can change from a rather sticky, putty-
like material to a brittle, leatherhard
state in quite a short time.

It requires a practised and delicate
touch; the pinching needs to be very
regular and even if the walls are to
retain a tension, yet be thin enough to
allow the light to pass through them
after firing. You will need to rest the pot
at more regular intervals. This usually
entails placing the pot upside down over

a suitable shape. (Some potters place a tennis ball in the top of a pot or plastic yoghurt pot and drape this with a soft separating material, for example tissue paper or muslin.) As the clay becomes firmer, the final pinching can be done, but great care must be taken as the porcelain becomes more brittle and fragile.

Any additions, such as a footring, must be joined at the leatherhard clay stage. A small coil or strip of clay can be added to the base. The surfaces to be joined can be moistened with a brush and the join reinforced by welding tiny coils of soft porcelain each side of the join with a modelling tool.

When dry, the forms need handling with great care, but it is at this stage that they can be scraped with a flexible steel kidney to refine the contours or to make the walls thinner and more translucent. It is possible to scrape patterns into the surface to allow the light to show through more in some places than in others. Sometimes holes are pierced through to allow the light to penetrate the walls of the form. I use dental tools for this more delicate work.

One cannot talk about pinched pots without referring to **Mary Rogers**. Although Mary Rogers had been handbuilding pots throughout the1960s, it was not until the 1970s

Tree Edged, Dry Valley porcelain bowl by Mary Rogers, 1975
Pinched and modelled, off-white crackle glaze
Courtesy of Buckinghamshire County Museum

Pinched Abstract Form by Mary Rogers
Courtesy of the Crafts Council

when she started to make her small pinched porcelain forms that her work was widely recognised. Her fine, delicate porcelain pieces, often with their wafer thin undulating edges, became extremely popular and much sought after.

Her pinched pieces were inspired by a wide range of natural forms and she translated the delicacy and translucency of such forms as flower petals, leaves and shells into clay. She often refers to the piece of dried marrow that inspired some of her early pieces. Unfortunately, many imitators have tried to copy the shapes without understanding the qualities of the natural forms and the personal exploration that preceded them.

Her pinched porcelain forms often had small footrings added and were scraped with a razor blade, when dry, to remove the fingermarks which Mary felt broke up the surface too much as the light fell across the forms. The decoration was done on the raw clay, often in the form of speckling or dappling in very subtle and natural colours.

Chapter Five
Coiling

Introduction

The need to make forms larger than was possible by pinching or by beating the clay, led to the development of a method wherein the wall of the form was extended by the addition of concentrically joined ropes or coils of clay. Coiling is one of the most versatile ceramic techniques and pots of enormous size and an amazing variety of shapes have been made in this way. It is not only pots that can be made using this technique, but also sculptural forms that range from human and animal to very irregular abstract forms.

Background

Examples of coiling can be found from all over the world, from superb African pottery with its lively decoration, to the huge, thickly coiled pots of the Mediterranean countries, used for storing oil and wine. Today many studio potters use the coiling technique to produce a wide range of pottery. Some work with great delicacy, producing finely finished and decorated pieces, whilst others produce forms around 5 or 6 ft (1.5 to 1.8 m) tall, architectural or sculptural in character. Contemporary potters have extended and developed the coiling technique, incorporating many different units of clay to build new and exciting forms; once again we must look back to the 1950s and 1960s, in

particular the work of **Ruth Duckworth**, to understand where this movement began. Although Ruth Duckworth only worked in Britain for a relatively short period before going to the USA, she was an important figure in transforming British studio ceramics. She went through a stage of making thrown tableware in stoneware and porcelain, but in 1960 she began making large coiled pots that were unlike anything being made at that time. They were heavy, thick-walled, asymmetrical forms inspired by organic shapes such as vegetables, fruit, pebbles and stones. They were earthy in colour with the texture of the clay showing between the glazed areas.

Clays for coiling

Most clays are suitable for coiling, and it is possible to use clays which are quite highly textured, which one cannot do when throwing. In fact, because of the greater thickness of the coiled wall, and the need for more mechanical strength, a lightly grogged clay is usually preferred. Heavily grogged clays give a natural texture to the surface, especially

Right
Coiled Pot by Ruth Duckworth, 1958
h. 195 mm w. 244 mm
Blue matt glaze applied on black slip with sgraffito decoration cut through glaze
Courtesy of Buckinghamshire County Museum

34

when scraped in the finishing stages.

In choosing a suitable clay, the size and shape, together with the decoration and firing temperature of the final piece, must be considered. It is also important to decide how much clay is likely to be needed for the pot and to prepare sufficient for the whole form. The clay should be carefully mixed and wedged to ensure that it is of an even consistency and free of air pockets. Because of the time taken to make a coiled pot, it is important to ensure that the prepared clay does not begin to dry out – it should be wrapped tightly in polythene until needed.

Making a coiled pot

A clear workspace with a good surface is needed for rolling the coils. You will also need a means of turning the pot while working, for example a turntable or upturned bowl, and a board or bat on which to place the pot. Brushes, and modelling, cutting and scraping tools may be needed, depending on the method used.

The base

Having made the decisions regarding size, shape, firing temperature and the most suitable clay, it is time to make the base. I have seen people make the base from coils, but this often proves unsatisfactory as the coils can unwind as they dry or cracks can appear. I think that it is best to either take a ball of clay and press it flat on a board or to roll out a sheet of clay. The base needs to be about the same thickness as the coils. It helps if the base is cut out accurately and any round object can be used as a template to mark the clay before it is cut out with a knife or needle. As it helps to turn the pot around, from this point onwards it is a good idea to place the

board on a turntable. If a turntable is not available, the board can be placed on a bowl or basin; this will enable the work to be turned at regular intervals.

Any join between two pieces of clay is a potential weakness and it is therefore important to make sure that the many joins of a coiled pot are well made. One of the weakest spots is the join between the base and the first coil. I would advise pinching up the edge of the base, creating a small ridge of clay to weld onto the first coil.

Making the coils

Rolling coils of clay often presents the beginner with unexpected difficulties, as the coil can become flat and misshapen. First of all, it is important to have a good, clear, flat space on which to roll the clay, as many problems are caused by not allowing sufficient space to prevent the ends wrapping themselves round other objects on the worktop.

It helps to squeeze out the piece of clay into a long shape before starting to roll the coil. When rolling the coil, the clay should be rolled over with a light pressure and a slight outward pull. Make sure that the clay turns at least a full 360° in order to keep it round. If the

clay starts to become oval then stop immediately and squeeze the coil back into a round shape before continuing. A porous work surface will absorb water from the clay as it is rolled, which can be useful if the clay is too soft. If this makes the clay too dry, the surface can be wiped with a damp sponge, which will help to return some of the moisture to the clay.

Mechanical aids can be used to make coils. Tools with a metal strip loop on a wooden handle, often sold as multipurpose tools, are very useful for making coils. By pulling them through a solid block of clay, coils can be cut through the block and then removed. This method gives a perfectly formed coil but the length is limited by the size of the block of clay unless a coil, larger in diameter than is needed, is cut and then rolled in the normal way to make it both longer and the correct thickness. Equipment, such as hand extruders, that can be fixed to the wall or the bench and will extrude long coils of clay that are even and ready for use, are available from suppliers of pottery equipment. Die plates can be attached to a pugmill, making it possible to extrude coils of

Rolling a coil by hand

Cutting a coil with a metal looped tool

different diameters, but these are not essential and can be expensive and take up studio space.

Joining the coils

When it comes to making coiled pots some potters like to make a stack of coils first so that when they start making the pot their rhythm is not interrupted. Others like to join on each coil as it is made, giving them time to reflect on the shape as it grows.

Whichever method you choose, the first coil must go on top of the base, not around the outside. If you have turned up the edge of the base, this clay can now be pulled up and joined to the outside of the coil. On the inside it is a good idea to work in the opposite direction and pull the clay firmly down from the coil to make the internal joint with the base. The end of the coil may need to be trimmed before being joined to the next, particularly if it has stretched. If a stretched end is not trimmed, it will start to make the pot bulge on one side, becoming more exaggerated as each additional coil is joined. When the coils are ready to be joined, the ends may be flattened, or cut diagonally to avoid a double thickness.

Coils are now added in concentric circles to build up the form. The form will be more controlled if only one coil is added at a time. Spiralling a long coil around several times, and then joining, can too easily cause the shape to be lost. If the clay is soft, the next coil can simply be placed on the previous one and the clay pulled firmly from one to the other to consolidate the wall of the pot. If the clay is not soft enough to make a good join, water or slip can be used to ensure that the coils adhere firmly. It helps if the clay is pulled and

smoothed in one direction on the inside and the other on the outside. It is also important not to let the ends be joined on the same side of the pot every time as this can make a weak spot. It is a good idea to smooth and finish the inside of the form as it is being made, as it may be difficult to reach all areas of the inside later.

Potters have different approaches to the outside. Some like to coil as much as they can before stopping to work on the outside, others like to smooth and check the outside contour of the pot after every coil. This is very much down to the temperament and approach of the

Joining the first coil inside the pinched up edge of the base

Adding more coils

individual. Batting with a paddle or beater can help to consolidate the wall of the pot as the coils are added. As with pinched pots, it is important to stop at regular intervals to allow the clay to stiffen enough to support the weight of the coils to be added. Not allowing the clay to stiffen is probably the cause of so many coiled pots collapsing or developing unsightly bulges. It is useful to have other pieces to work on during the course of coiling a pot.

The shape of the pot is controlled by positioning the latest coil on the one below. To close in a form the coil needs to be placed on the inner side of the rim of the pot; to open the form it should be placed on the outer edge of the rim. As coiled pots have a tendency to stretch outwards it is a good idea, if you want the form to go straight up, to keep the coils slightly on the inside of the top. To make a narrow neck or top the coils will need to be thinner, and if sudden changes of direction are to be made, such as from the shoulder of the pot to the neck, it is important to ensure that the clay has stiffened enough to support the newly added coils. Various tips are suggested for supporting a pot in danger of collapsing, such as packing it with screwed-up newspaper or inserting a polythene bag of the appropriate size and filling it with a granular material like sand or sawdust. This can be poured out once the clay is firm enough to support itself, and the bag pulled out. Strips or bands of supporting material can be wrapped around the outside to prevent the walls collapsing. These tips are useful to know in an emergency, but if the coiling is not rushed and the coils are allowed to dry sufficiently before adding new ones, such problems should not arise.

The rim

The rim of the coiled pot, as with all pots, is very important and therefore requires a more studied statement. It is the culmination of the vessel, linking the inside to the outside. The form must not look as if it has just stopped, but should have a distinct termination that makes the pot look complete. This can be achieved by a change in direction, such as opening out the top of the pot with the last few coils, or by making the final coil thicker. It can also be shaped, flattened, or made more angular in section with the aid of a hacksaw or Surform blade. A cut template in a rigid material, like card or plywood, can be held against the rim as the pot is turned, to ensure a regular and even top.

Batting the form to improve the shape and consolidate the clay

Using a Surform blade to shape the rim

adding flattened coils on the inside edge of the top. These are smoothed on and then, at intervals in the making process, she bats the surface with a wooden paddle, compacting the clay and also thinning the wall. She feels this is also important in defining the contour of the form and giving it life and an organic quality. When the completed form is leatherhard, the surface is slightly roughened to allow a brushed coating of slip to adhere. The layers of slip (usually about three layers) are burnished with the back of a spoon. The pots are low fired to about 950°C (1742°F), in order

The surface

The surface that comes naturally from the texture of the clay or the rhythmic joining of the coils is often in character with the form. Accentuating the thumb marks, or using a particular tool to join the clay, will give a regular textured pattern to the outside surface. If a more precise or refined contour is required, the surface can be scraped with a tooth-edged tool – an old piece of hacksaw blade is ideal. The toothed edge will cut through the bumps and fill in the hollows until a more regular surface is achieved; it helps to work in different directions. The texture that results from the scraping can be kept or, if a smoother finish is required, a tool with a smooth edge can be used to give the final result. Any decoration in the clay itself, such as incising or impressing, must be done while the clay is still soft or leatherhard.

To a potter like **Gabriele Koch**, the surfaces of her beautiful and sensual coiled forms are an integral part of the making and firing processes. She uses a mixture of clays to make a grogged body and builds up from a pinched base, by

Burnished Vessel by Gabriele Koch, h. 37 cm
Photograph by Heini Schneebeli

Burnished Vessel by Gabriele Koch, h. 34 cm
Photograph by Heini Schneebeli

Right
Three Very Tall Vessels With Lines by David
Roberts. Coil built and raku fired

to retain the polished surface, before being smoked in a metal dustbin or drum of sawdust. This gives a rich, soft surface patterning, but does not distract from the fine tension of the contour.

David Roberts has developed a very personal way of handbuilding that relies greatly on his ability to raku fire his large coiled pots, but this does not detract from the quality of his coiling. He uses a white textured clay, called 'T' Material, but sometimes adds up to 50% porcelain clay. He extrudes his round section coils and builds his pots in the traditional way, carefully placing the coils to follow the subtle changes of direction he wishes the form to take. The

coils are pressed down quite hard and pinched a little to produce pots of great precision and thinness. Once the coiling is completed, the pot is scraped with a metal kidney and then smoothed with a rubber kidney, followed by burnishing with a metal spoon. Two layers of slip are then added, and burnished in between layers. Depending on the decoration, lines might be incised

through the slip before the biscuit firing at 950°C (1742°F). Layers of glaze and slip are often added before the raku firing, and the pots removed from the kiln while still hot, and placed on a bed of sawdust inside a metal drum. The carbon in the smoke penetrates wherever the clay is not protected, including any crazing lines in the glaze. The excess carbon is removed and then the surface is polished with various abrasives. Finally, some forms are polished with beeswax.

The large garden pots of **Monica**

Young provide another example of the relationship between surface texture and form. She uses the heavily grogged crank body and rolls her coils by hand, joining them in the traditional way. She checks the diameter of her pot at regular intervals as she coils, to ensure that the contour she requires is being followed. Because of the size of the forms (2m/6 ft) and the weight of the clay, Monica Young often finds it necessary to use bandages to support the walls of the pot as the coils are being added. Long-handled paddles are used to beat the walls on the inside, to keep the fullness of the contour.

When the form has reached the required height, the tops and edges are reinforced with more clay and shaped and smoothed. As it dries, the surface is finished with a Surform blade and then rubbed with sandpaper to bring up the gritty texture. Finally the whole pot is rubbed with blackboard chalk, helping to bring up a rich toasted colour in the 1300°C (2372°F) firing.

Controlling the drying process

In order to control the drying of the clay, thin polythene bags or sheets can be either tied tightly around the parts of the pot that are to remain workable, or loosely draped around the form to allow it to dry slowly. It is possible to use hairdryers, fan heaters or even a blow torch to speed up drying. I have heard of potters who lower lightbulbs into their pots, or candles on tin lids with wire handles, in order to build up a gentle heat inside the pot to help the drying. However it is generally better for the beginner to avoid all attempts to hasten the drying by artificial means, as this can cause uneven drying and cracking.

Below
Round Vessel with Lines by David Roberts
Coil built and raku fired

Right
Monica Young coiling in her studio

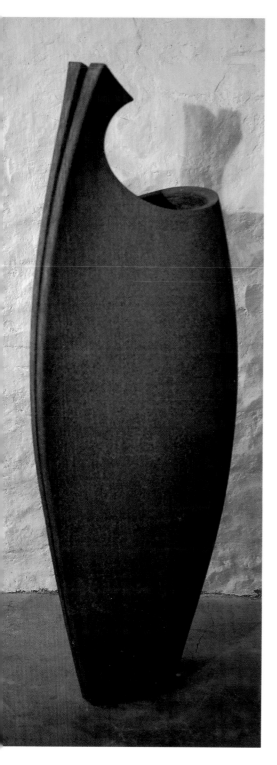

Wendy Hoare, who is a sculptor by training, builds her pots using the traditional methods of joining coils of clay, as described above. She starts working at eye level and gradually moves the pot to lower levels as it grows, in order to focus on the joining of new coils, and to reach inside. As part of the making, she works on the outside with a variety of scraping and patting tools, and on the inside with a child's rubber ball, which helps to retain the tension of the wall. She finds the rubber ball 'kinder' to the clay than a hard tool. Many of her pots are large (up to 1 m/39 in. tall) and are concerned with form and surface textures, based on natural forms. Decoration is minimal, using only slips, stains and oxides to enhance the finished work before firing.

Alternative methods of coiling

I have outlined the traditional method of coiling using the rolled, round coil, but there are a number of alternatives that are used by coilers. Flattened coils or strips of clay, cut from a rolled slab of clay, can be overlapped and squeezed and smoothed onto the wall of the form. Small discs or patches of clay can be used as the unit to build up the wall of the pot. Instead of using a round coil, some potters pinch their coils into a triangular section and pull the corners down each side of the coil below. Each of these methods gives a different character to the form. Some have a very thin wall which undulates; some will show a linear strata around the pot, reflecting the nature of its making. It is not always necessary to completely join the coils or

Large Coiled Pot by Monica Young

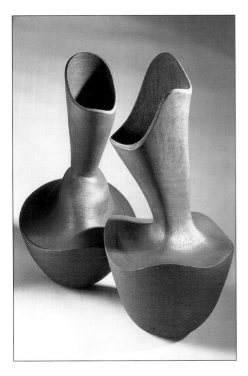

Pod Pots with Stalk Necks by Wendy Hoare, h. 90 cm. Coiled

Preparing a flattened coil

Joining a flattened coil on the inside of the top

to join them in regular horizontal layers; they can rise, leaving spaces to form an undulating landscape with glimpses into the interior space.

Combined coiled forms

As with other techniques, composites can be made with coiled forms and different methods combined to good effect.

For smaller pots, or when starting, a thumb pot may make an excellent starting point to which coils can be added. Similarly, the final coils can be pinched very thinly to change the character of a form and alter the final outcome of the coiled pot. **Betty Blandino** is a potter who often works in this way. She sometimes starts with a ball of clay, pulling and squeezing the walls up from a hole in its centre. Sometimes a mould is used to support

the shape as the walls are pinched higher, and coils are then added until the final shape is achieved. The walls of the pot are often worked until wafer thin, and some forms are finished with extended pinched tops that enhance the lightness and upward movement. Most of her forms are asymmetric, and the surfaces enhanced with coatings and rubbings of white slip and oxides. Her pots have a quiet modesty about them, and to those who think that coiled pots must be heavy and robust, Betty Blandino shows how light and fine a coiled pot can be.

More complex pottery forms and animal and figurative shapes can be created by coiling from two or more bases; after careful spacing of the hollow shapes the gap can be bridged by coiling across, and when the forms are joined the coiling can continue upwards. It is possible to change direction with coiling by adding coils on one side only, until the opening is facing the direction required, and then the coiling can continue in the normal way, as for the neck of an animal, for example.

Jill Crowley is a potter who has used the coiling technique for a whole range of forms that show great perception and humour. They include bust portraits of bald, middle-aged men, cats' heads on black plinths, mermaids and, recently, a series of hands inspired by the chubby hands of her children when they were very young. Some of these hands have been made into humorous teapots.

The heads are coiled up, in the traditional way, from the shoulders or

Coiled Pot by Betty Blandino, 1996 h. 30 cm

Right
Coiled Pots with Pinched Tops by Betty Blandino, 1996 h. 23 cm

47

neck, but the rounder hand forms are initially coiled and rested in a round mould to support them, then the coiling continued until the main form is completed. The fingers are made by wrapping sheets of clay around cardboard tubes or dowel rods. When the soft clay tubes are removed from the supports they are then pressed and folded into finger shapes and joined onto the coiled hand forms.

Some of her work is fired in a raku kiln, but other pieces are fired to stoneware temperatures. Colour is an important part of Jill Crowley's work and she uses a range of slips and underglaze colours. The warty speckles on the portraits are achieved by using a red grog in her clay which melts at higher temperatures.

In the early 1970s a new group of women potters emerged from the Royal College of Art, to establish a new direction in ceramics. In particular, **Elizabeth Fritsch** was to make an immediate impact and enjoy wide popularity. Although potters like Ruth Duckworth had done much in the 1960s to make handbuilt pottery more acceptable, their work was heavy, robust and usually brownish in colour. Elizabeth Fritsch was to change that with her finely coiled pots, pinched and

Left
Jill Crowley working in her studio

Below
Blue Hand by Jill Crowley, 1996
Photograph by David Cripps

Above
Trio : 1. Vase from Tlon, 1984 2. Lachrymatory, 1987 3. Vase Double Fault 1988 By Elizabeth
Fritsch. *Photograph by David Cripps*

Right
Blown Away Vases with
Collision Particles
by Elizabeth Fritsch, 1994

scraped until they appeared to be so thin that it was difficult to relate them to what had previously passed as coiled ware. They are made in a grogged white clay and the surfaces painted with layers of coloured slip. The geometric surface patterns are altered physically and optically by the changes in the contour of the form. The shapes are often flattened and lacking in a true third dimension, but by a combination of the shape and the optical illusion of the surface pattern she gives her work what she calls 'a two and a half dimensional appearance'.

When coiling, Elizabeth Fritsch works very slowly and uses flattened coils to build up the form. In her recent 'Sea' or 'Wave' forms, flat slab-like facets are coiled as part of the elaborate shapes. The sharp corners are achieved by cutting the coils at the edges, and making the corner with another join in the coil. The groups of 'Wave' and

Sea Piece by Elizabeth Fritsch, 1998

'Tower' pieces together relate to capture wave movement and architectural forms. In much of her work the influence of her early musical training can be seen in the precision, rhythms and patterns.

Gordon Baldwin is one of the most influential and original British potters of the second half of the 20th century. He has used a variety of techniques including throwing, slabbing and press moulding, but coiling has been the basis of much of his work, and is his main technique at the time of writing. He began handbuilding in the 1950s and has used whatever method is most suitable to execute his ideas, which are derived from landscape, his great interest in music, and also influenced by Surrealism and the artist Jean Arp.

Gordon Baldwin uses a clay called St Thomas's Oxidising Body, which he finds 'very accommodating'; he extrudes coils about half an inch thick which he joins in the traditional way. The wall is batted and thinned more at edges, or

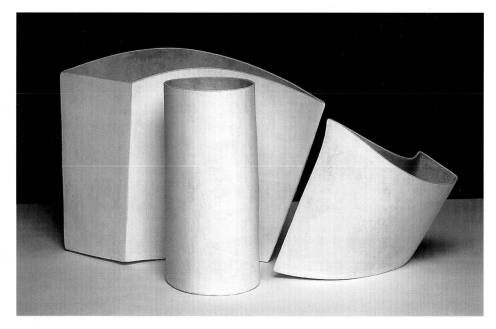

sometimes left thicker to reinforce an opening. He enjoys coiling because it allows freedom to change shape or direction. Forms are often made separately, like large pebbles, and then openings cut to join them together so that they appear to fuse or merge together. The openings in these 'Fusions' are luted with slip and welded together. 'This is all part of a process of adding and subtracting, piercing and hole making until the final structure emerges.'

His work is mainly black, white or blue. The dry white surface is created by many thin layers of white slip, with firings between applications. The white pieces have drawn or painted lines worked into and onto the surface in an abstract design. Some forms have what appear to be very random edges or marks, but these are usually highly controlled, often being reworked many times. Some of his sculptural forms take months to complete, with as many as six or seven firings. His work is fired to earthenware temperatures, usually about 1070°C (1958°F), but the pieces become more vitrified through repeated firings.

Left
Blue Vessel by Gordon Baldwin, 1997
Photograph by Philip Sayer

Right
Cloud Shape by Gordon Baldwin, 1996
Photograph by Philip Sayer

Below
Cloudscape Bowl by Gordon Baldwin, 1998
Photograph by Philip Sayer

Chapter Six
Slab Building

Introduction

I have always found the versatility and potential of working with sheets and slabs of clay an exciting challenge, both creatively and technically.

All slab building starts with a basic sheet of clay, after which the imagination and creativity of the potter must take over. The form might be anything from a flat tile to a soft wrapped form or a hard-edged clay box. The soft, plastic, flexible qualities of the clay can be exploited, or the clay can be left to stiffen, and used to make regular hard-edged forms. Making pots with stiff slabs of clay has been likened to joining sheets of metal or pieces of wood, while working with soft slabs has been compared to origami, pattern or dress making, as the shapes are cut out and then bent and folded to fit together. The similarities are obvious, but by the very nature of the material, slab-built clay forms have a distinctive character of their own.

Slabware not only has great potential in the range of forms possible, but also offers, in its flat surfaces, considerable opportunities for decoration and enrichment in all the stages of making and firing. Unfortunately, this technique can also lead to more faults and technical problems than most other methods. For this reason I will describe in detail the methods most likely to ensure success.

Historical background

There are many historical examples of flattened slabs of clay being used to construct a wide range of artefacts. These range from prehistoric sarcophagi and aquamaniles to dishes, plates and boxes of all descriptions. In architecture, slabs of clay have been used to protect and decorate the outside of buildings in the form of roofing and wall tiles. Internal floors and walls of many of the world's greatest buildings have been richly decorated with tiles.

In their book *Twentieth Century Ceramics*, Rice and Gowing state that while Ruth Duckworth was primarily responsible for making coiling and pinching techniques acceptable in the post-war period, it was **Ian Auld** who made slab building acceptable.

He was certainly influential both as a potter – concentrating for nearly 20 years on making slabware – and as a teacher, especially at Camberwell School of Arts and Crafts, where he was Head of Ceramics for many years.

Many of Ian Auld's pots are in the form of rectangular slabbed bottles with coiled necks. Although they have a simple architectural quality they are, like much of the handbuilt stoneware of the 1950s and 1960s, heavy and made with a grogged clay which, when combined with certain glazes, often resulted in a rough, dry, sandy surface. Although Ian Auld has not produced much pottery since the 1970s, the piece illustrated is fairly recent and has been made with a softer slab to give a greater fullness and softness to the form.

Clays for slab building

Most clays can be used for slabware, but it is important to select a clay that is appropriate for the size and thickness of the slabs. Heavily grogged clays are not suitable for thin slabs or for sheets that will be too sharply bent or curved. Porcelain and similar clays are not suitable for larger forms.

The softness and flexibility of the clay is important, and choosing the most suitable state of flexibility or rigidity is

vital. The clay must be soft enough to ensure a good join, but rigid enough to keep the shape.

Making slabs of clay

There are various ways of making slabs or flat sheets of clay. The usual method is to press or beat the block of newly wedged clay out on a cloth or piece of material that will prevent it sticking to the work surface. The clay is then rolled with a wooden rolling pin. It helps in this process to turn the clay over at regular intervals, partly because it sticks to the cloth or surface and becomes difficult to roll, and partly to stop it becoming compressed on one side only. It also helps to roll from the centre of the slab towards the edge at this stage, as this enables the clay to spread more

Slab Pot by Ian Auld

Above
Rolling a sheet of clay between lath strips

Below
Cutting clay slabs with a wire bow or harp

Below
Alternative placing of slabs on the base

easily as it becomes thinner. When the clay is nearly of the thickness required, two wooden lath strips of the actual thickness required for the finished slab can be placed on the bench on each side of the clay. By resting the ends of the rolling pin on the lath strips and rolling up and down, the clay will be rolled to an even thickness. If any air bubbles appear as the clay is being rolled, they can be pricked with a sharp tool to allow the air to escape. Many slab builders, such as Alison Britton, regard the rolling out of the slab as an integral part of making a slab pot.

Another method of making slabs of even thickness is to use a tool called a bow or harp. This tool has a wire stretched between two arms. The wire can be moved up or down the notches on the arms to allow for different thicknesses of clay to be cut. A simple homemade version of this can be made by having two wooden rods with notches cut equally at regular intervals up both rods. A wire can then be stretched between the two. It is necessary in this technique to have a wedged block of clay and to set the wire to the thickness required, cutting through the block and then moving the wire to the next notches and pulling through again to cut another slice or slab. This can be repeated until the whole block has been cut into slabs. This method is really only suitable when smaller slabs are required.

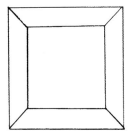

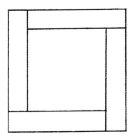

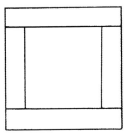

Other methods range from repeatedly banging or throwing a lump of clay onto the bench or floor until it is suitably flat and of an even thickness, to pouring slip onto a plaster bat and letting it stiffen into a thin sheet of clay. The slip method is usually used to make a thin sheet of porcelain. As with the making of coils, it is possible to buy equipment for slab making. This consists of a bench with rollers that press out large sheets of clay at a pre-set thickness.

When the slabs or sheets have been made they should be placed flat with sheets of newspaper between them to prevent them from sticking together. If they are going to be used straight away they can be taken from the stack as required, but if they are to be used for hard or rigid slabbing then they need to be left for a while to stiffen. The newspaper will not only stop them sticking together, but will help to dry out the surface of the clay evenly on both sides. A board or heavy flat weight (a kiln shelf is ideal) will help to keep them flat. Tiles or slabs will curl up or warp if allowed to dry more on one side than the other. Keep some of the same batch of clay in the soft state for joining the slabs together.

When cutting the slabs into the sizes required it is important to think ahead and plan where the overlaps of the butt joints will be, and to allow extra clay on your measurements for these. It will require approximately the thickness of the slab to be added where each butt joint arises. Decide how the sides will relate to the base. I think that it is better to build on top of the base so that the whole form can shrink together and avoid the possibility of the sides cracking away in the drying. This means that the base has to be cut large enough to accommodate the widths plus overlaps (thickness of the slab). Corners can be made by cutting the edges of the sides to make a 45° mitred joint, in which case the measurements of the base will

Cutting out shapes

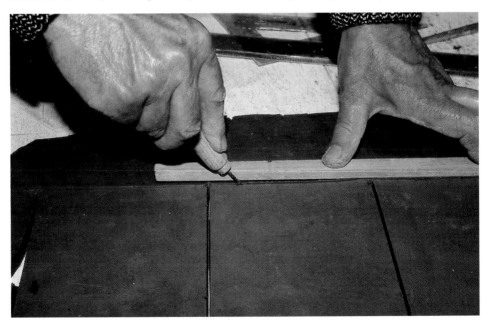

correspond exactly with the width of the sides. Edges can be cut to 45° by chamfering the edge with a Surform blade. It helps to place the slab near the edge of the bench to do this. When the planning has been completed, the clay can be placed flat on a board and the shapes cut out with either a narrow bladed knife (which will tend not to stick to the clay as much as a table knife) or a cutting needle. With regular, angular shapes it helps to cut a straight line first and then work from that, using a plastic or metal ruler and set square. If curves or circles are required use a round lid or object as a guide. When complicated shapes are needed or the shapes are to be repeated, then templates can be cut in card or plywood. To make a rigid box-like form, the slabs need to be stiff enough to stand up on their own yet soft enough to make good joins. With most clays this will be a stiff leatherhard state. If the cut out shapes are still too soft, they can be placed flat on a board that has been covered with a fresh sheet of newspaper and another sheet used to cover them.

A board can then be placed on top to keep them flat until they are ready to be joined.

Joining the slabs

It is important that the joins in slabware are well made, as they have a tendency to crack apart in the drying and firing stages. I have developed the following method for joining the stiffened slabs for box-like forms. First of all I score or scratch the edges or parts of the slabs that will form the join, with a crosshatch of lines. This can be done with any pointed tool, but I find that using an old table fork is the quickest tool to use. Some potters then wet these

scratched areas or coat them with slip or slurry made from some of the soft clay that was kept aside. I find that to dip an old toothbrush into water and brush the bristles over the scored area not only moistens the clay, but the brushing creates slip from the clay itself. Potters develop their own methods of preparing the surfaces to be joined. Some have a tray of water and dip the scored edges into this before pressing them together. Sometimes these wet areas are slid up and down against each other to create their own slip. The two prepared surfaces can then be pressed firmly together. It further strengthens the join if the clay from the inside corner made by the two slabs is notched or pulled together with a modelling tool. This helps to weld the clay from the two slabs together. A small coil of clay can be pressed into this inside corner and smoothed into the sides. This not only strengthens the join but also makes it neater and less likely to collect dust and dirt with later use. Some potters add the coil when all the sides have been joined to the base, but I prefer to do this as I

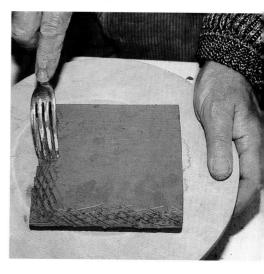

Using a fork to score the area to be joined

Brushing the area to be joined with a wet toothbrush to make slip

Brushing the edges with a wet brush to prepare them for joining

Placing the first slab on the base

Pushing a thin coil of soft clay into the corner to reinforce the join

join each slab and while the join is easily accessible. Always support the outside of the slabs when pressing from the inside, to stop the joins from pushing apart. Usually this can be done with the hand as you work along the join, but it might be necessary to use a brick or board to support the whole slab while assembling. I sometimes find that a tall form is better constructed on its side.

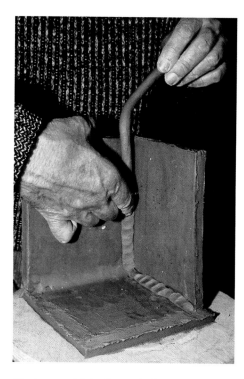

Placing a coil into the vertical corner

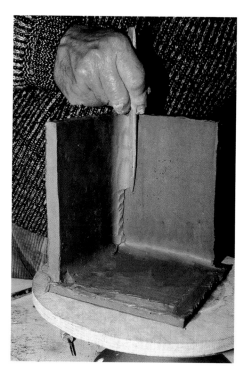

Smoothing in the coil with a modelling tool

When all the inside joins are completed, the outside of the joins can be considered. If the clay has pressed firmly together and the slip has sealed the seams then the join might be left or even become a feature of the form. To ensure a good join I usually notch the clay together along the seam and then smooth the clay over the join. This can be neatened later, when the pot is at the leatherhard stage, with a Surform blade. The angularity of the shape can be strengthened by gently batting it with a flat piece of wood. This will also help to consolidate the joins.

When the form begins to dry to the stiff, leatherhard stage, the sides can be further refined by shaving them with a Surform blade (this is best taken out of the holder). It is also possible to avoid very sharp corners that might be prone to chip by gently chamfering them to take away the sharpness without losing the angularity. Slabware needs to be allowed to dry slowly to avoid uneven drying and cracking. When it is completely dry, the final rubbing down and finishing can be done with a sheet of plastic kitchen-pot scourer or sandpaper.

This basic method of joining slabs or sheets of clay can be applied or adapted to suit most types of slab building.

Alison Britton, like Elizabeth Fritsch, was one of the key potters to emerge from the Royal College of Art in the early 1970s. After a training in which she studied all the basic techniques she was drawn towards making slabware, which gave her the opportunity to combine the painted two-dimensional surface with the three dimensions of the assembled form. A short time was spent making and decorating tiles before she began to produce pots based on the jug form. The jug form offered her the type of shape that could be used to explore her love of planes and edges, and had different viewpoints that could be interrupted by the lip and handle. Alison Britton has now moved on to forms that she just calls 'containers' and these have included a broader exploration of forms.

She uses a basic buff stoneware clay body which is fired to temperatures around 1100˚C (2012°F). This helps to keep the warmer colour of the buff, rather than the grey of the higher temperatures.

Her clay is beaten and rolled out by hand on a thick marine canvas, which she says does not rot as other fabrics do. The slab is turned regularly until she is satisfied that the thickness, evenness and surface is what she requires. Sometimes

Square Pot by Alison Britton, 1996

White jar by Alison Britton, 1998, h. 49 cm w. 33 cm d. 31 cm

dry clay dust is rolled into the surface of the clay to break up the overall uniformity and then both sides are scratched, impressed, trailed and painted with slips. The two sides are never the same. Alison Britton likes to work with leatherhard slabs, but if any pieces need to be curved, they are propped up while the clay is soft.

When they are ready she starts to cut the slabs, taking account of the painting on them, and as the pot is constructed a kind of dialogue develops between the two and three dimensions. The slabs are joined in the traditional way and reinforced with small coils on the inside of the join. More recently the containers have had coiled tops which has softened the upper form and the top edge.

More painting is applied to the finished pot, with slips, and after the biscuit firing a third layer of painting is added using underglaze colours. If after the glaze firing, which takes place at about 1100°C (2012°F), Alison Britton is not satisfied, she adds more painting in underglaze colours. These are mixed with a gum solution to help them stick to the glaze until the pot is refired.

Lidded boxes

The basic box structure can also be developed to create a wide range of forms, many of which may require lids. The box can be made to whatever size and shape by the method described above, and the lid can be made in one of many ways. Probably the simplest is to cut a slab that will fit exactly on top of the box. Small strips of clay will need to be joined to the underside, forming a flange that fits into the top of the box, preventing the lid from slipping off. A knob or means of lifting the lid can be added, or alternatively, the lid can be

Cutting the lid with a needle while the clay is still soft

Lifting the lid after cutting

made to overlap the top, making it easier to lift the lid itself.

Another method, which I have often used myself, requires the top slab to be joined, making a completely enclosed box. The walls of the box are then cut through with a needle, at an appropriate distance from the top, while the clay is still soft. The line of the cut can be angular or undulating like a landscape. When dry the lid should locate exactly and not slide off.

Three Slab Boxes with Cut Lids by
Michael Hardy

Soft slab forms

Many potters prefer to exploit the pliable
qualities of soft slabs. This can be done
simply by bending and curving the slabs
after they have been cut, but this is
usually only possible with smaller slabs.
A potter who uses soft slabs on a larger
scale is **Mo Jupp**. He tells how, as a small
boy, he watched his mother, who was a
seamstress, cut patterns and sew the
fabric shapes into a garment. He thinks
of his use of soft slabs as a form of
pattern cutting and joining.

Most of his work is based on the
human form and has ranged from
helmets to female figures. He manages
to capture with great skill the subtle
movements of the female form, from the
curve of the back as the truncated arms
reach up to stretch, to the changes in
direction of the standing figure as the
weight is placed on one foot. All of this is
achieved by bending and joining soft
slabs in a very free way that retains the
quality of the clay. Some of his latest
pieces are in the form of columns, but
are still based on the female form. These
are made by wrapping clay around a
pole, in sections, using a technique
similar to that described below for
making cylindrical forms. When they
are stiff enough to be removed they are
dried and fired. They are finally
assembled on a rod to make the 'Female
Icon Forms'.

Regina Heinz is another potter who
cuts and tailors her slabs to produce her
soft and rounded box forms. She usually
starts with drawings that are often based
on landscapes. These are then

Twisting Figure by Mo Jupp

Right
Female Icon by Mo Jupp, blue glaze and gold leaf

Below
Waiting Figure by Mo Jupp

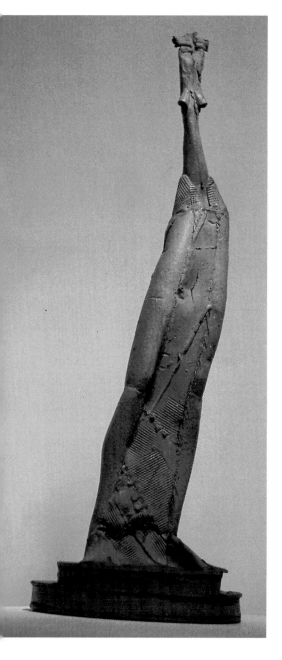

transferred and developed on the sheet of rolled out clay. The slabs of clay are cut and shaped to relate to the marks and drawings on the clay surface. She waits until the clay is no longer soft, but is still pliable enough to bend and shape. The slab of clay is then shaped over a support of chicken wire netting and screwed up newspaper. When it is leather hard it is removed from the wire support and the other side is made in the same way.

The first shaped slab is placed upside down and filled with screwed up newspapers to act as a cushion when the two slabs are brought together. The small side walls are then cut and tailored to fit exactly before they are joined to the two large slabs. The completed form is then scraped down with a metal kidney tool and finally smoothed with a plastic kitchen-pot scourer.

Regina Heinz uses either a Crank or White St Thomas's clay body for her forms which are then biscuit fired to 1060°–1080°C. The biscuit fired pieces are then painted with oxides and glazes and fired to 1020°–1040°C. After the first glaze firing areas are masked off and further painting takes place. An underfired Lithium based glaze is used which gives a very lively speckled quality.

Lake Wall Piece by Regina Heinz, h. 35 cm w. 43 cm d. 5 cm

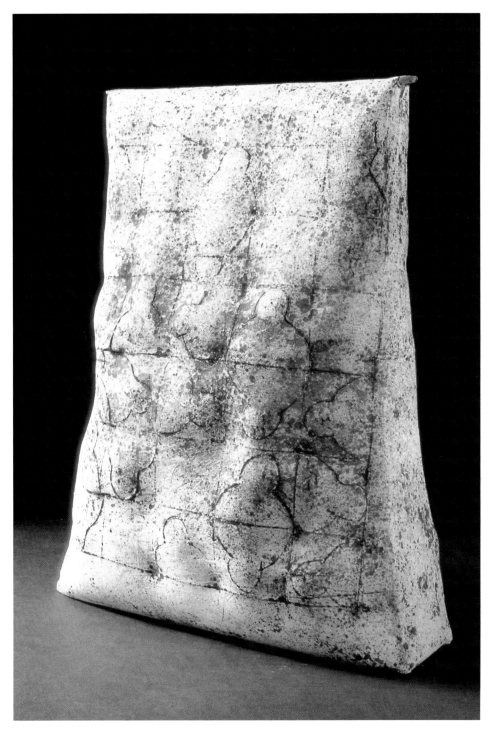

Dream Image by Regina Heinz, h. 50 cm w. 20 cm

Impressing patterns and textures into the clay slabs

Sheets of clay can be enriched with patterns and textures whilst still in the soft state. This can be done after the clay slabs have been assembled, but quite often it is done as part of the process of rolling the slabs.

The clay can be rolled over surfaces or materials that will leave an impression in the clay itself. Impressions of hessian, corrugated card, bubble plastic and other such sheet materials are often used. Jill Crowley rolls clay over rubber car mats to pick up the pimply impressions. Similarly, if rolled over granular materials such as sand, grog or sawdust, these materials will be impressed into the surface of the clay to give a textured surface to the slab. Some

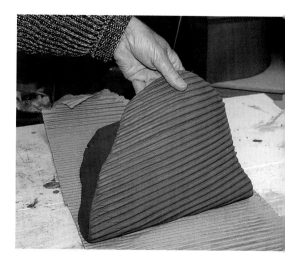

Impressing a pattern into a slab of clay by rolling it onto a sheet of corrugated card

Below
Detail of Blue Torso by Carol Greenaway

Wrapping a sheet of clay round a cardboard tube which has been loosely wrapped in newspaper

Making the join down the side of the clay cylinder

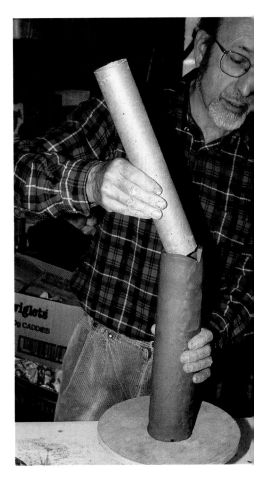

Cutting out a base from another sheet of clay

Right
Sliding the cardboard tube out of the newspaper sleeve when the clay is stiff enough to support the shape

will remain embedded in the clay, but others, like sawdust, will burn away in the firing to leave a pitted surface. The range of materials that can be used in this way is endless, but beware of materials that might give off toxic fumes when in the kiln.

A more controlled use of this technique is where the materials or objects are carefully placed on the surface and pressed or rolled into the sheet or slab of clay. **Carol Greenaway** decorates and enriches her sheets of clay in this way before assembling them in their soft state to make her torsos and figurative pieces. She uses a white stoneware clay and makes her slabs on a slab rolling machine. She mainly uses fabrics to give her slabs a 'textile connotation'. This also suggests the link between the body and clothing. Her slabs are freely joined and the form is built up from the base, bending the slabs into shape and pushing and stretching from the inside to accentuate the contours. The forms are finally ash glazed and fired to 1265°C (2309°F).

Cylindrical forms

Larger and more elaborate curved shapes will need some support. A cylindrical form is often made by wrapping a sheet of soft clay around a rolling pin or cardboard tube. It is always important to wrap a sheet of newspaper around the supporting shape first, to prevent the wet clay from sticking; it helps to use pieces of adhesive tape to stop it unrolling. Two edges of the sheet of clay are cut at right angles, forming the base edge and one of the upright edges. The rolling pin or tube is then placed horizontally on the sheet of clay, which is wrapped around the support and rolled until the position

for the second upright edge is determined; the other edge is then cut. The two edges to be joined are flattened to avoid a double thickness when overlapped and welded together. The form is then stood upright on another slab of clay, upon which the base of the tube is marked. After cutting out the base, it is joined to the cylinder. The rolling pin or cardboard tube is left to support the clay until it is stiff enough to support its own weight. It must not be left too long or the clay will shrink and become too tight for the support to be removed; it may even crack. If the separating newspaper has not been wound too tightly around the supporting shape, it will allow the pin or tube to slide out easily, leaving the paper sticking to the clay. This can usually be peeled away from the clay fairly easily, but if not can be left to burn away in the firing. The irregular top of the cylinder can be left as it is or trimmed. Additional work can be done by pinching, coiling or even adding thrown shapes.

Pre-shaping slabs

Some more elaborate curved shapes are easier to handle if they are pre-shaped and allowed to stiffen a little before being assembled. Slabs of soft clay can be draped over shapes or into hollow forms to give regular or irregular forms. The clay must always be separated from the object by newspaper or a thin cloth if there is any danger of it sticking. Sometimes the sheet of soft clay can be simply shaped by draping it over cardboard tubes or screwed up balls of newspaper. Jill Crowley has pressed sheets of soft clay on the inside of cardboard boxes to make the bases for her 'Cat Heads'.

Left
Two Slab Bottles by Michael Hardy, 1993
h. 65 cm and 30 cm
Coiled necks and pre-shaped curved tops

Above
Cat Portrait by Jill Crowley
Showing a base made as a box pressing
Photograph by David Cripps

Have A Heart by Philippa Cronin

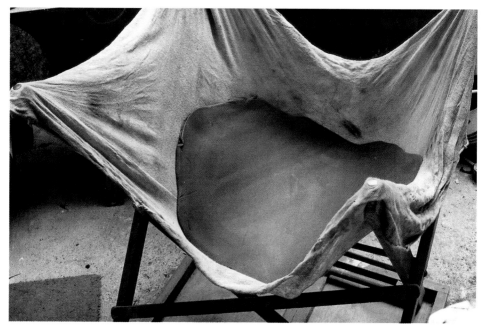

The Hammock method of pre-shaping a sheet of clay

The hammock method

A sheet of clay can be left on the cloth on which it has been rolled and this can be slung by pinning or nailing the edges to the top of a wooden box, suspending the cloth and clay inside. An alternative is to tie the corners of the cloth to the legs of an upturned stool or table. The clay will then stiffen into whatever shape the cloth falls.

Philippa Cronin is a slab builder who had previously worked with metal. This clearly influenced her early work which was very angular and hard edged. Her slab-built forms have changed over the years, as she has continued to explore the interaction of forms and planes. The surfaces and edges have been curved and beaten to modify the angularity. Her most recent forms are double-walled, curved shapes, concerned with the relationship between internal and external space.

Philippa Cronin uses a white body called 'C' Material and the forms are constructed with two slabs held apart by an internal structure of clay ribs. As the curves are created, coiling is used to span the space between the edges of the two slabs, completely enclosing the space between them. The surfaces are painted with slips, oxides and stains before and between firings.

August by Philippa Cronin

Chapter Seven
Press Moulding and Slipcasting

Introduction

Moulds have been used to shape clay from the very earliest times. It is known that clay was smeared on the inside of baskets and that the baskets were burned away, leaving the hardened clay shape. Primitive man used anything, such as a pebble or rock or even a hollow in the ground, that was suitable to keep the soft clay in shape until dry enough to keep that shape unsupported. Traditionally, moulds were made of wood, stone or fired clay, but later plaster of Paris was used. Simple clay moulds from early civilisations have been found in many countries around the Mediterranean, and in China and the Americas. Moulds are used to hold the soft plastic or liquid clay slip in shape until the clay is stiff enough to support itself. They can be simple one-piece hollow moulds or multi-piece moulds of great complexity, requiring great skill and knowledge to make and use. Most of the everyday mass-produced ceramics, such as tableware, sanitaryware and many electrical components, are made in moulds.

Because of this association with repetition and mass production, the use of moulds has not always appealed to the studio potter, who is concerned with the making of individual pieces. The use of moulds has been seen as an indirect and rather sterile way of using clay, as opposed to the more direct and expressive forming methods and techniques. As a result, some potters were only prepared to use moulds for making dish shapes, but in more recent years potters have learned to make more creative use of press-moulded and slipcast forms. Mould making, using the cast and pressed forms, has become part of the creation of new combination pieces. Quite often moulds are used to make the additions that are to be part of a larger, handbuilt form. **John Berry** press moulds some of the figures that sit on the top of his teapot forms and **Kate Malone** uses moulds to produce the repeated units that make up the surface of her fruit and vegetable pots. Sprigged reliefs, such as those seen on her large coiled teapot, can also be made in moulds. Many of my own handbuilt forms have press-moulded or slipcast additions that are related to the human form.

Reference has already been made to the different objects and materials that have been used to support the clay until it is stiff enough to maintain its required shape. The clay used in this way also often reflects the surface or shape of the support. Box pressings and hammock shapes are good examples of this.

Press moulding or slipcasting is a more precise way of shaping clay. The clay comes into contact with the inner or outer surface of the mould and retains that shape. The concave surface of a mould determines the outer surface of the clay form and the convex surface is used to produce the inner surface.

Clays for press moulding

Most clays can be used for moulding, but obviously the finer the clays the more precisely the details are reproduced. With press moulding, the consistency of the clay is important if it is to capture all the details of the mould. The clay needs to be soft enough to press into all the details, but not too wet and sticky or it will take too long to dry and may be difficult to successfully remove from the mould. On the other hand, if the clay is too stiff it will be difficult to press fully into the mould and may crack in the process. The making of purpose-made casting slip will be discussed later.

Moulds

As stated above, the first moulds were made of wood or stone and later of clay that had been biscuit (bisque) fired. The plastic clay was pressed into these shapes and as the porous surface of the mould absorbed the moisture from the clay, the shape slowly began to shrink away from the mould and was released. Although these methods can still be used, most moulds are now made of plaster of Paris. Ralph Daniels is credited with introducing in Staffordshire in 1740 plaster of Paris moulds for casting pottery forms.

Simple shapes can be made in one- or two-piece moulds, but more intricate shapes need multi-piece moulds that can be taken apart. It is important that the cast clay form can be released easily from the mould and is not trapped by overhangs or undercuts. Simple forms that are wider at the open end of the mould can easily be made in a one-piece

mould, but a completely three-dimensional form will require at least a two-piece mould.

Making a plaster of Paris mould

The mould is made from a master or model of the required form. The model is usually made of clay, but plaster of Paris, or an everyday ready-made object can be used. If plaster is used, a block is usually turned on a potter's wheel or lathe, for a symmetrical shape, or carved or sledged and smoothed for an irregular shape. A clay model is usually made solid and similarly may be turned on the potter's wheel, or a shape can be modelled by hand. It is also fun to cast from 'found' objects like polystyrene or plastic packaging, egg boxes, pieces of tubing, boxes, or simple forms like light bulbs or bottles. Parts of the body can also be cast. It is, however, important to ensure that these can be released easily from the plaster and that the plaster will not stick. A releasing agent like petroleum jelly will be needed.

Making a one-piece mould

The model for a simple dish or bowl mould can be made solid and is inverted. The mound of clay is built up on a smooth board that allows a space of about 7.8 cm (3 in.) between the rim of the form and the edge of the board. The rim or circumference of the shape can be drawn on the board as a guide. A round shape can be turned on the pottery wheel, but other shapes need to be modelled and contours made even with the help of profiles or templates cut from a piece of card, wood or plastic. It is better to let the clay harden a little before smoothing and burnishing the

Clay model with wooden profile used to make the shape

Mixed plaster of Paris being poured onto the model with a clay wall to retain the liquid plaster

finished surface. It is worth spending extra time on the original model before casting, in order to save time spent working on each cast or pressed form later.

When you are satisfied with the model, and before it becomes dry, a wall or cottle needs to be built round the shape, to contain the plaster. Wooden casting boards can be made with angle brackets on each corner that allow for adjustment. Sheets of thick card or linoleum are very useful for round shapes and these can be tied and held in place with string. All of these materials will need the seams sealed with soft clay to prevent the liquid plaster seeping out. A wall of clay can be made by rolling out sheets of clay to about 18–25 mm (0.75–1 in.) thick, then cutting out walls that are at least 40–50 mm (1.5–2 in.) above the top of the clay form. Again, all seams need to be sealed, and if there is a danger of the walls being pushed over by the weight of the liquid plaster they should be buttressed with extra clay.

A solid clay model of a dish ready for moulding

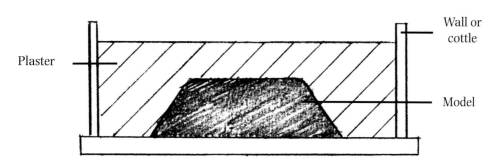

A cottle or clay wall is placed around the clay model and liquid plaster of Paris is poured over the inverted dish shape

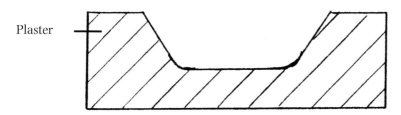

Plaster of Paris mould with clay model removed

Moulds for sprigged decoration

Although this book is not about decoration, reference has been made to sprigged reliefs on handbuilt forms. Probably the best known example of sprigged decoration is that of Wedgwood's Jasper Ware.

With sprigged ware, the motif is modelled in relief on a board, usually modelled larger than the size required for the final piece in order to facilitate the modelling of the details and to allow for shrinkage. This is then cast as for a one-piece mould, as described above. When the mould is dry, clay can be pressed into the mould, left for a short time and then the blade of a knife moistened and pressed onto the clay and the motif lifted out. This is then joined onto the leatherhard surface of the pot, with the aid of water or slip if necessary. If the sprigged motif needs to be reduced in size it can be repeatedly fired and remoulded until it is much smaller, and the detail finer.

Making a two-piece mould

To make a simple three-dimensional shape, a two-piece mould will usually be needed (although it is possible to make a cylinder in a one piece mould). Again a model has to be made, usually as a solid form. It is then necessary to decide where the seam between the two parts of the mould will be, to avoid any undercutting. This line needs to be carefully marked on the form. It is then placed level on a pad of clay and more clay is built up to the line and carefully worked to a smooth finish. It is important to follow the dividing line very precisely. A wall is built around the embedded form as for the one-piece

mould. The plaster of Paris is mixed and poured over the exposed part of the model. After about half an hour the walls can be removed and the embedded form turned over so that it sits on the block of plaster. The clay is removed from the other part of the form so that it is now partly encased in a block of plaster. Locating 'keys' or 'natches' are made in the smooth surface of the plaster mould, to ensure that the two halves of the mould fit together correctly, or natches can be made in the outer edges. These can either be made by twisting a round shape into the plaster to make a hollow, or by cutting notches with a Surform or hacksaw blade into the edges. The plaster surfaces now need to be coated with a separator; petroleum jelly, soft soap, oil or a clay wash can be used, to prevent them sticking together. Any marks or damage to the exposed part of the model need to be repaired before new walls are placed around the plaster and model, making sure that the top of the wall comes at least 5 cm (2 in.) higher than the model. Again make sure that any seams are sealed with soft clay. It is now possible to mix a new batch of plaster and pour the second half of the mould.

When the second pouring of plaster has set, the walls are removed. When the plaster is hard enough, the two halves of the mould are carefully separated. If this proves difficult, let a tap drip onto the seam until it parts. Do not attempt to force the parts of the mould apart by banging the plaster or with tools. If it still proves reluctant to separate, leave it overnight and then try again when it has had time to dry a little more. Once separated, the model can be removed and the mould cleaned with a sponge and then allowed to dry thoroughly. Do not attempt to speed up the drying on a radiator or kiln, as this can affect the plaster and shorten the life of the mould. The two parts of the mould can be located together using the 'keys' that were made in the plaster. They must then be held firmly together with string, strong rubber bands, or bands made of sections of a tyre inner tube.

Found materials and objects can be used to shape clay that is pressed into or over them. I have found that to make a mould of an everyday object can be a very good way for students or beginners to understand the principles of mould making. Many plastic objects have been made in a mould themselves and the seams are clearly visible, so can be followed when making moulds from them (for example, plastic bottles, balls and toys). All of these objects will need to be well coated with a separating agent (grease, oil, petroleum jelly etc). There are times when, because of a surface texture, it could be very difficult to separate the original from the plaster. In cases like this, it might be better to take a clay pressing which could be biscuit fired and then used as a bisque mould.

Coiled Teapot with Sprigged Decoration by Kate Malone, 1998, h.50 cm, w. 84 cm

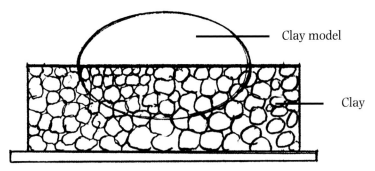

Clay model

Clay

Clay is built up to the line and carefully worked to a finish

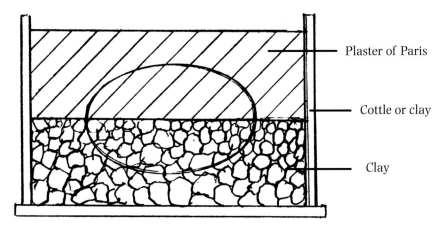

Plaster of Paris

Cottle or clay

Clay

A wall is built around the embedded model and plaster of Paris is poured over the exposed part of the model

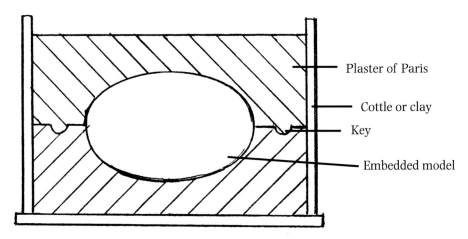

Plaster of Paris

Cottle or clay

Key

Embedded model

The embedded form is turned over so that it now sits on the block of plaster. The clay is removed and locating keys made in the plaster surface. The plaster surface needs to be coated with a separator and a new clay wall built before the second half is poured

Mixing the plaster

Fine white plaster of Paris of dental quality is best for mould making and can be purchased from a pottery supplier.

It is best to mix the plaster in a flexible polythene bowl or basin, as this will allow you to flex the bowl to crack out any set plaster left after pouring.

Half fill the container, making sure that there is enough mix to cover the model with a layer of about 38–50 mm (1.5–2 in.) above the highest point. Always sprinkle the plaster lightly into the water, avoiding lumps. If the quantities are to be measured by eye, the plaster should be sprinkled until the heap appears above the surface of the water to form an island. If you prefer to weigh the plaster use 800 g to 0.5 litres of water (1 lb 12 oz plaster to 1 pint water). To avoid creating air bubbles, stir gently by moving the hand around the bottom of the bowl until all the lumps have been dispersed. The plaster is then ready to pour over the model (do not let the plaster start to thicken in the container or it might not reach all the corners or details). Gently agitate the mixture to release any air bubbles trapped around the model and then, after levelling the top, allow to set. The plaster will set quite quickly, but needs to be left for between half an hour and one hour, before the containing wall is removed. It is wise to remove the clay model a little later in order to avoid chipping the still moist plaster. The outside of the mould can be trimmed with a knife or Surform blade to remove corners and fragile edges. It then needs to be left to dry in a warm atmosphere for several days before use. Do not attempt to force dry the mould on a kiln or heater as this can damage the plaster.

Safety

It is important to keep all plaster away from clay that is to be fired. The clay that has been used for the model or for clay walls or seams should be kept in a separate container. Any small piece of plaster will damage a pot if it is in the clay when fired. Plaster will also clog sinks and drains. Utensils that need to be cleaned or washed should be dealt with in a separate bowl or bucket.

Press moulding from a one-piece mould

The usual method of taking a pressing or cast from a press mould is to roll out a sheet of clay and press this into or over the mould.

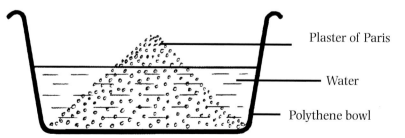

Plaster of Paris

Water

Polythene bowl

The plaster should appear above the surface of the water to form an island

A sheet of clay pressed into a dish mould and the excess clay being trimmed with a wooden modelling tool

The clay is rolled out to an even thickness on a cloth or canvas as for slabware. The thickness varies according to the size of the form, but for the average size dish (about 30 cm or 12 in.) the clay will need to be about 1 cm or 0.5 in. thick.

When the clay has been rolled out to a size larger than the size of the mould it can be picked up on the cloth and draped, clay side down, in the mould. It is always better to lift the clay on the cloth to avoid stretching or tearing. Once the clay sheet has been placed in the mould it is easy to peel the cloth away from the clay. Always make sure that the sheet of clay is large enough to overlap the edges, as it can weaken the form if patches have to be added to fill any gaps. The sheet must be smoothed and pressed gently but firmly against the surface of the mould, using a sponge or rubber kidney tool. Do not use your fingers, as this will leave grooves and marks on the surface.

When the clay is firmly in place, the excess can be trimmed using a wooden or plastic tool, unless an irregular border is desired. Do not use a metal blade or knife, as this will cut into or scrape away the plaster at the edge of the shape. Give the surface a final smoothing and think carefully about whether you want the edge of the dish or form to have a flat cut edge, or whether it needs to be rounded. Whatever you decide, the rim or edge needs to be finished with great care, as I have found with students' work that many excellent and well decorated dishes are spoilt by badly finished edges.

The dish needs to be left in a warm atmosphere until it can be seen to be shrinking away from the surface of the

Right
Moulded Piece by James Tower
Made by joining two press-moulded sections
Photograph courtesy of Buckinghamshire County Museum

mould. Again it is better not to try to speed up the drying by using other sources of heat. When it appears to be ready, a board can be placed over the top and the board and mould can be turned upside down and the mould gently lifted off, leaving the dish upside down on the board, like a jelly on a plate. It is better to let the dish stiffen and dry in this position to avoid warping as it dries out. Some potters place a layer of butter muslin in the mould before placing in the sheet of clay, in order to ease the removal of the pressed shape.

The procedure for taking a cast or pressing from a hump or mushroom-shaped mould, with a convex surface, is much the same except that the clay is draped over the mould. If it is a deep shape it is important to remove it before it shrinks tightly onto the form and cracks.

For deeper or more complicated steep-sided moulds, it may be necessary to press the clay into the form from a lump. Start at the centre in order not to trap air, and work towards the edge. If the clay is too thick, any excess can be removed with a wire loop tool. The usual tools such as rubber kidneys and sponges can be used, but to reach more inaccessible places a sponge can be tied onto the end of a stick.

It is impossible to talk about the use of press moulding as part of the making of handbuilt forms without referring to the very distinctive sculptural vessels of **James Tower**. These were made by joining two press-moulded shapes to a

Torso Form by Peter Lane, w. 40 cm
Made by a combination of press moulding and handbuilding

bivalve shell. These were usually in tin-glazed earthenware and decorated in black and white.

Peter Lane is a potter better known for his thrown pots, but he also makes very fine and sensitively crafted handbuilt forms. He uses press-moulded shapes to form the two halves of his slab-built 'Torso' forms. The shapes are pressed one at a time in the same mould and are then joined, cut and shaped, using slabs or coils of clay to complete the form. Many of the forms are decorated with subtle geometric patterns created by repeated masking and air brushing.

Press moulding from a two-piece mould

To press mould from a two-piece mould, the two halves have to be filled separately using the same method as for a one-piece mould. The main difference comes when the excess clay is trimmed, as the clay needs to be trimmed to leave a projection of about 6–12 mm (0.25–0.5 in.) above the plaster edge. These projecting edges of clay are then either moistened or coated with slip, and the two pieces of the mould pressed together. The excess clay will sometimes prevent the two parts of the mould meeting completely, but often this does not matter. If it does matter, then it is possible to make a channel or space in the mould as a space for any excess clay to collect. If it is possible to reach the

Three Heads by Christy Keeney, 1999

Flat Head by Christy Keeney, 1999

inside of the seams it helps to weld these together.

Once the form has been left to stiffen, the mould can be opened and the form removed. Excess clay on the seam is trimmed and smoothed.

Christy Keeney is an Irish potter who makes a simple two-piece mould of the basic shape of his figurative moulds. From this mould he then presses the basic form, using a Crank clay body which is later covered in a white slip. He adds clay to complete the shape and then draws into the surface to produce the features. Manganese and copper oxides are worked into the drawn lines and colour is added in the form of underglaze colours and vanadium pentoxide. After the biscuit firing at 1040°C more colour is added and they are finally fired at about 1120°C.

The faces and heads show an astute observation and a great attention to detail. They have expressions of piety which Christy Keeney describes as being between happiness and sadness.

Slipcasting

Slipcasting works on the principle of the porous, absorbent mould absorbing water from the liquid clay (slip), leaving a coating or skin of the plastic clay on the mould surface. When the excess slip is poured out of the mould, a thin layer of clay remains on the mould surface. As this dries out it slowly separates from the mould and can be removed. Slip casting obviously allows for much thinner and lighter cast forms to be made. It is also capable of reproducing much finer detail.

The moulds can be the same as for press moulding, but because they are usually used for more precise casting, plaster of Paris is the usual mould material. The main difference is that in the case of two- or more piece moulds, an opening is necessary to allow the slip to be poured in and out; this needs to be placed where it will not interfere with the shape to be cast. The opening is made by including a plug of clay or 'spare' when the mould is being made. After the plaster has been poured, the clay plug is removed and this becomes the pouring hole. Whereas press moulds are usually shallow or open forms, allowing for the easy removal of the pressing, this is not a problem with a slipcast form, and the mould can be much deeper and more detailed, but it is important to remember to avoid undercuts.

Slip

Slip is made when clay is mixed with water. Pieces of clay (it is easier if the clay is dry or powdered) are dropped into a container, half filled with water, and left to soak. This rough mixture of clay and water is called slurry. The slurry is passed through an 80-mesh sieve to produce a mixture, the consistency of thin cream, which is known as slip. These water slips, which usually consist of equal parts of water and clay, are often satisfactory for simple casting, but they are more likely to settle, shrink and warp when used in more complex moulds.

Deflocculated Slip

A good casting slip needs to keep the particles of clay in suspension, give good definition when casting, have minimum shrinkage, yet have good strength when dry. All of this needs to be done without excessively saturating the mould.

To make such a slip the potter needs

to understand that the particles of clay or slip are naturally drawn together, an attraction usually known as 'flocking'. To change this, the potter can either add more water, which produces a liquid suspension (but also makes for some of the problems listed above when casting complex forms), or make what is known as a 'deflocculated' slip. A deflocculated slip is made by adding a substance known as an electrolyte, usually an alkali in the form of sodium silicate or soda ash. This changes the electrical charge that causes the particles to be attracted and flock, instead making them repel one another and float apart. Thus the slip is more fluid in consistency but with a smaller water content. This deflocculated slip will not then saturate the mould, allowing it to be re-used more quickly, and will eliminate many of the faults that occur when casting the more complex shapes.

The main disadvantage of using a deflocculated slip is that the plaster mould deteriorates more quickly and definition may be lost. A fungus-like growth may appear as the electrolyte is absorbed, but for the artist potter who wishes to produce a limited number of casts this is not usually a problem.

Once the basic technique of slipcasting is understood, a whole range of variations can be tried that can include colouring the slips with slip stains or metal oxides, adding grogs, sands, sawdust or even paper pulp. When using slips it is also possible to work at a wide range of firing temperatures and types of firing.

Casting slips can be bought from suppliers, ready made in plastic containers, but if potters wish to make deflocculated slips of their own, some recipes are included below. I would suggest that some tests and experiments

are made first, to find a slip that suits your needs, with finer adjustments being made as you become more familiar with the slips and their uses. The ingredients should be weighed carefully and in a dry state, and added to the recommended quantity of water. The sodium silicate and soda ash should be dissolved in hot or warm water (taken from the total amount specified), and slowly added to the water. Always store slip in airtight plastic containers.

Recipes for deflocculated slip

Earthenware Casting Slip
1100°C (2012°F) (parts by weight)
- 40 Ball clay
- 15 China clay
- 17 Cornish stone
- 28 Flint
- 0.25 Sodium silicate (140 TW grade)
- 0.20 Soda ash
- 35–50 parts by weight of water to every 100 parts by weight of powdered material

White Non-Translucent Porcelain
1250°C (2282°F) (parts by weight)
- 30 Ball clay
- 220 China clay
- 125 Feldspar (Potash)
- 125 Flint
- 1.3 Sodium silicate
- 1.3 Sodium carbonate
- 0.22 litres of water

A potter who takes the industrial slipcasting technique and combines it with a studio based approach is **Jessie Higginson**. Her simple, cylindrical and flat forms are slipcast and then worked and decorated by hand to make them all individual pieces. Another potter who combines the repetition of the

Large Flat Vase by Jessie Higginson. Slipcast form individually hand finished

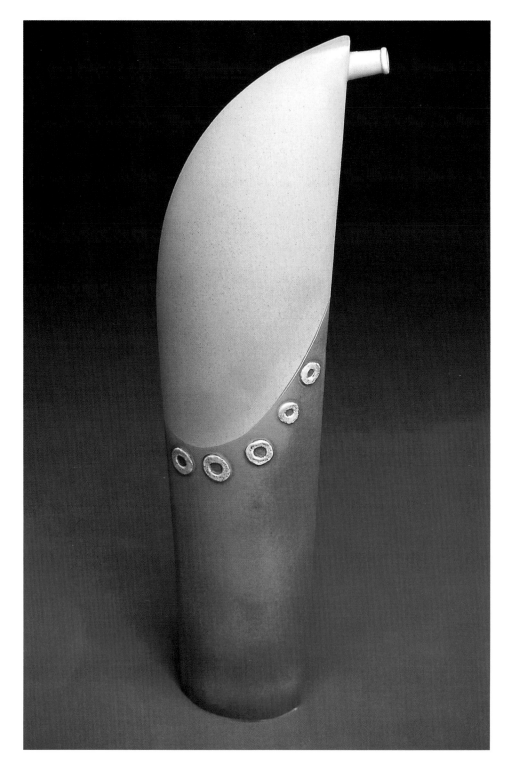

slipcasting process with handbuilding methods to create her individual forms is **Kerry Miller**. She uses a range of slipcast shapes to construct her elegant and streamlined forms.

Developing the casting process

I have described the basic techniques used when making simple moulds and pressing and slipcasting from them, but in order to develop the expressive and imaginative qualities of the forms it is sometimes necessary to experiment and exploit unforeseen accidental effects.

The clay could be pressed or poured into a mould a little at a time, perhaps using different coloured clays or slips. The units could be pellets, strips or irregular torn pieces of clay. The slip could be dribbled or trailed into the mould using a slip trailer. Other materials could be pressed into the mould, to mask or create open shapes or thinner areas in the cast form. A thin cast shape could be taken from a mould when still soft and distorted to meet an expressive need.

The ability to repeat the shape many times offers possibilities for composite forms constructed by the joining of numerous similar forms.

Left
Arc Bottle by Kellie Miller
Assembled slipcast forms individually worked and decorated

Chapter Eight
Combining and Developing Handbuilding Techniques

With the handbuilt ceramics of the postwar modern movement came a greater freedom of form and a change in attitudes to the handling of clay. Many potters working today have no fear of breaking with the traditional ways of using clay. They see themselves as artists who happen to work in clay, and have developed and extended the traditional making methods to translate concepts into a real form or object. Their approach is often to just 'make' pieces using whatever technique is appropriate or expedient.

Combining techniques

It is not unusual for several techniques to be used in one piece. This can produce many problems, as it is always difficult to produce all parts at the same time, in the same state of wetness or dryness. The clay needs to be stiff enough to give rigidity and strength, while at the same time being moist enough to allow a good join to be made. Varying thicknesses can lead to uneven drying and be a cause of cracking and warping. Care must be taken to keep each part at the required consistency and in the workable state described in the chapter on clay. It is also easy, when adding pieces, to create

Left
Hand Form by Michael Hardy
A combination of slab building, coiling and slipcasting

pockets of trapped air which will also cause cracking or even shattering when fired. A network of holes or openings, made as the piece is being constructed, will allow the air to expand freely.

An early way of combining techniques was to extend a pinched form by the addition of coils, and many potters today, like Gabriele Koch, start their coiled pots by pinching a bowl shape. The reverse is also true, where a coiled pot is pinched, to thin it or to change the character of the form, as in the work of Betty Blandino and Ursula Morley-Price. Slabbed box-like forms, such as those made by Ian Auld, often have coiled necks to make them into bottle shapes and to contrast the roundness of the coiling with the angularity of the slabs.

In order to achieve the freedom of form that he requires, **John Berry**'s pots are assemblages that make use of a combination of coiling, slabbing and press moulding, to create his lively and often humorous teapots, tureens and bottles. He uses either Crank mixture or 'T' Material or a mixture of both. His slabs are made on a slab roller and his coils extruded and, where necessary, he also press moulds parts for his pots.

A series of drawings is made first, which he sees as an intermediary stage between the idea and its realisation in clay. The pieces are worked on over a period of time, being painted with slips and oxides and underglaze colours at

Early One Morning by John Berry, h. 39 cm w. 36 cm

different stages of the making and firing. They are often fired several times, starting at stoneware temperatures and reducing the temperature at each successive firing until, in some cases, enamel painting and an enamel firing bring the piece to completion.

John Berry's teapots appear to have their roots in the 19th-century Staffordshire tradition, but one soon becomes aware of the influence of 20th-century abstraction in the shapes and the expressive use of colour and brushwork.

Thrown sections are used by some potters in conjunction with handbuilding. This again calls for very careful timing, to allow the wet thrown sections to reach a state where they can be worked and joined with the plastic clay used for the handbuilt elements. In the construction of his bird forms, **Peter Lane** starts with three thrown sections that are altered and beaten into the

Waiting for Adam by John Berry. h. 35 cm w. 45 cm

Stoneware Birds by Peter Lane
A combination of throwing and
handbuilding

shapes of the body, tail and neck. Coils
and flat sheets of clay are added to
complete the form and, when
leatherhard, they are further refined by
much scraping with flexible steel
kidneys. After the biscuit firing various
combinations of oxides are sprayed on
and partially brushed off when dry.
They are finally spray glazed and fired to
stoneware temperatures in an electric
kiln.

For **Delan Cookson**, the softness and
plasticity of clay is an ideal material for
interpreting the qualities of the
everyday objects that he uses as subjects
for his sculptural pieces. The objects are
often tools that serve some basic
function such as squeezing or
tightening. When interpreted in clay by
Delan Cookson they take on a new
meaning. He uses Crank mixture to
make the combination of slabbed and
thrown elements which are put together
with a minimum of what he calls
'interference' modelling.

Kate Malone's large and richly
coloured fruit and vegetable forms
appear to be in the tradition of the
works of Thomas Whieldon and Bernard
Palissey in the 18th century, yet she is
the maker of decorative ware that is
very much of the 20th century. Her
organic forms have a vitality and
sensuous quality that come partly from
the scale of much of her work and

partly from the intensity of her crystalline glazes.

Kate Malone is basically a coiler, but often uses moulds to press some of her smaller shapes. She press moulds the 'baby fruits' as well as the additions with which she builds up the surfaces of her forms. She also sometimes starts with a thrown shape and then completes the form with coils. The surface of the form is then built up with either hand modelled parts, like leaves, or press moulded units that are repeated to give the surface patterns of the fruit.

Quite often she starts several similar pots at the same time and explores variations on her theme with each one. She uses 'T' Material which gives her a white base for her coloured glazes and which is also very tolerant of the

Toothpaste Tube by Delan Cookson
Slabbed and thrown

repeated firings (some pieces are fired up to ten times). This clay is used for both her earthenware, which is high biscuited to 1180°C (2165°F) and glazed to 1060°C (1940°F) and also for the stoneware which is biscuited at 1000°C (1832°F) and glazed to 1260°C (2300°F).

Developing the techniques

Over time, the techniques themselves have been developed. Coiling has involved the building up of the form using a wide range of units, from flattened strips or bands of clay to torn pieces. Clays of very different types have been used together. This has quite often made for a very exciting surface as some have melted more than others, but the different shrinkage can also lead to cracking and warping. These faults, which would not be acceptable in a

Above
Nut and Bolt by Delan Cookson
Slabbed and thrown

Right
Kate Malone working on Pineapple Forms

functional object, can often be acceptable in an artefact that is more a piece of sculpture. The form may still resemble a vessel, but is clearly not intended to contain anything. The spaces between the strata or layers of clay allow light to pass through, linking the internal and external spaces. The form becomes an object made to stand in its own right, and a different set of aesthetic criteria is needed to appreciate such a form, than would be used when looking at a functional pot.

Experiments such as the addition to the clay of a wide range of materials, have resulted in some very exciting new forms and surfaces. Some will add texture to the clay body, like grog, sand or ash, others will burn away in the firing like sawdust, paper pulp and vermiculite (see the chapter on clay). These change the mechanical strength of the clay, making it more open and porous, altering the appearance of the clay surface, and allowing the structures to be thicker.

Above
Adding the surface patterns

Below
Joining pineapple leaves

102

Pineapple Form in the kiln

Laminating clays

The technique of laminating or sandwiching different clays together takes many forms. As described in the chapter on clay, different layers of clay can be alternated before kneading and wedging to ensure a thorough and even mix, but if only partially wedged or rolled together, like a Swiss roll, then the different coloured stratas of clay remain. If sliced across the layers, these agate-like pieces can be placed in a mould and held in place with a backing layer of slip or clay. Another type of laminating process is achieved by pouring slips or spreading soft clay onto a porous surface, like plaster of Paris or an absorbent paper, and rolling a sheet of clay onto it to pick up the veneer or thin layer from the porous surface. This can be repeated to make a sheet of clay with layers like plywood.

Another method is the one used by **Ewen Henderson**, who has probably done more than any other British potter to extend the boundaries of ceramics. He switched from throwing to handbuilding in the 1970s, and was soon to develop unique ways of handling clay. He began to make thin asymmetrical coiled pots with rough and textured surfaces. His approach is totally experimental and his early pots were as much an exploration of clay, fire and starting points as the making of vessels. Although he is obviously inspired by the landscape, and more recently by megalithic circles, the clay itself, to a large extent, is his main inspiration.

In much of his recent work he has been obsessed with 'edges, points of change and endings' as well as a concern for 'the significance of what is broken, torn or cut'. Contrasting qualities are very important aspects of his work, where fullness and flatness or compression and expansion are important features.

In his coiled pots Ewen Henderson extends and develops techniques by using different clays in the same piece, clays which all behave in different ways when fired. They crack and bubble or become pitted or melt as a result of the addition of such materials as sawdust and silicon carbide and as a result this often gives a surface reminiscent of a geological specimen. In order to control

Left
Large Vessel by Ewen Henderson, 1992
h. 61 cm
A mixture of bone china and porcelain
laminated onto a stoneware clay with
colouring oxides and silicon carbide added
Photograph by David Cripps

Below
Zig Zag Form by Ewen Henderson
h. 60 cm w. 60 cm
Paper and clays laminated together, formed
in a sandwich of blotting paper printed with
ceramic colours
Photograph by David Cripps

the variations in the clay he begins to layer or laminate the clays on to a core clay, which makes them less likely to crack and separate, giving them more stability. Ewen Henderson also adds colouring oxides and stains and paints on further layers of slip to give great sublety and depth to the surfaces of his forms.

His work has become quite large and like very rugged and beautiful sections of landscape or rock formation. The increased size has created more technical problems which he has tried to overcome by incorporating wire structures into his forms as support. As he found, it is important to use Kanthal or Nichrome wire as ordinary galvanised wire gives off extremely toxic fumes.

He has also experimented with composite clays. He uses a paper clay made up of a ratio of 30% paper pulp to 70% clay slip. This allows him to make a form in a number of pieces which can be worked separately before being joined. It also allows him to change surfaces, add thin sections, fill cracks and alter and redefine edges, even after numerous firings.

Ewen Henderson pushes materials to their limits, almost revelling in the accidental effects, which he uses and controls to make some of the most original and exciting ceramic sculpture today.

Sara Radstone is another potter whose work is at the sculptural edge of ceramics. Her forms increasingly resist classification and have been described as a 'kind of non-form'. She has slowly simplified and abstracted from vessels to

bag- or sack-like shapes, through to horizontal boxes and forms that lean against the wall, and small wall shapes that are exhibited as a series, in a line.

She is concerned with volumes, but the openings have slowly changed to small slits to make the volumes into hidden interiors. Her thin walled forms look fragile and brittle and at the same time strong and rock-like. Although, at first, her pots appear to have an organic quality there is also the influence of crushed and discarded obsolescence found in the urban environment. Her surfaces are inspired by the deterioration of the torn and tattered walls, hoardings and other neglected and discarded surfaces found in the city. Her surfaces are textured and pitted and reveal the dimple marks left by her fingers. Sara Radstone builds the walls of her forms with small slabs or patches of clay about 2 or 3 in. square (5–7.5 cm). These are squeezed and pinched onto the previous edge to slowly make a thin wall that encloses the space inside. Even the thin, propped wall pieces are still hollow. The dented, knobbly, pinched surface that comes from the making is retained and further worked with oxides and slips, which are rubbed to further reveal the texture. The glaze is also rubbed and scratched before the glaze firing.

Some of the pieces are now too long for her kiln and have to be made in sections and joined with chemical metal adhesive after firing.

Mixed-media ceramics

Dipping absorbent materials in slip or liquid clay is not new; usually the fabric or material burns away, leaving a delicate fossilised clay replica. This was often done with lace, hessian or paper doilies and has been extended to more

Left
Buttressed Form by Ewen Henderson, 1988
h. 61 cm
Laminated clays

Left
Triptych by Sara Radstone, 1998
Photograph by Philip Sayers

Above
Two Forms by Sara Radstone, 1998
Photograph by Philip Sayers

solid cellular forms like sponges, but again care must be taken during firing as fumes will be given off. Fibreglass matting and tissue can also be used in the same way, but in this case the glass fibre melts and remains part of the clay, giving it a greater strength. When the non-ceramic materials are dipped in the clay slip they can become saturated and lose their shape, often needing support until the slip stiffens. This can be a temporary support, such as a rod or wire over which the wet matting or tissue can be draped, or a permanent wire or metal structure built into the form that will withstand the firing temperatures. Kanthal or Nichrome wire is most suitable for this. I have used

plaster of Paris moulds to shape slip soaked fibreglass matting (see p.8).

Gillian Lowndes is a ceramicist whose work is closer to sculpture than pottery and is at the forefront of these innovative ways of working. Her work has ranged widely and she has demonstrated a great ability to assimilate change. She uses clay as her principal means of expression and has concentrated on handbuilding techniques. She made pinched pots for her first exhibition at the Primavera Gallery and has enjoyed the creative potential of coiling. The material is the important thing in her work, and she has had to overcome many problems as she has pushed at the limits of what can be done with clay. Experiments with

Almost Off The Wall by Gillian Lowndes, 1998

Right
Sieve, Scroll and Fork by Gillian Lowndes, 1998

materials help to develop her ideas, and then begins an interplay of materials and ideas that leads to the creation of some of the most original and exciting ceramic sculpture being produced at the present time. Non-ceramic materials are incorporated into the clay and much of her work can best be described as assemblages.

Gillian Lowndes has regularly made forms that use fibreglass matting or tissue dipped in a porcelain slip, some of

which had to be supported with a structure of wire. Her 'Brick Bag' series incorporated housebricks wrapped in bags of slip-impregnated fibreglass matting and held together with wire. She also tried to use foam rubber soaked in slip, but found the fumes during firing unacceptable and had to find alternative methods to make the forms. More successful were her slip-impregnated loofahs which, when fired, fossilised the fibre of the plant material. These were joined with wires to become wall-hung pieces.

Gillian Lowndes has used a broken, industrially made teacup which she has coated with a clay mixture and then assembled, and she has also used springs and pieces of tile. Many of these constructions are so complex that they have to be assembled a little at a time, involving repeated firings. Often the process starts with firings at stoneware temperatures, to achieve the qualities that can only be achieved at that level, and the subsequent firings are at lower temperatures to allow more delicate pieces to be added, or low-temperature colours to be used.

Combining metal with clay

Metallic additions or structures can be used either to strengthen the clay when it is being stretched to its limits, or to bring a contrasting material or form into the work. In some of her latest work Gillian Lowndes has combined her slipped fibreglass matting scrolls with everyday metallic objects like a sardine can and tablespoons and forks, and the wire that had previously been used structurally now plays a more important and visible role in the ceramic

Scroll by Gillian Lowndes, 1998

sculptures. Sometimes the metallic additions are fired with the ceramic to high temperatures in order to make them melt and distort, but in some pieces they are added at a later stage. The different metals used have different melting points, and experiments and tests need to be made if excessive melting is not to ruin the ceramic and possibly the kiln.

Egyptian paste

Low-temperature clays like Egyptian paste can be useful as coatings for found objects or as a means of holding things in place. Gillian Lowndes has used Egyptian paste for her coil and wire pieces and as a support for some of the scroll pieces.

Egyptian paste is an early form of glaze and was developed before 5000BC. It consists of a combination of the glaze and body materials and, as the clay dries, the glaze materials move towards the surface of the paste and remain there. When fired, a thin layer of glaze develops on the surface. A variety of colouring oxides and stains can be added but a very popular one is copper oxide, which gives the rich turquoise colour that one associates with many Egyptian pieces. A recipe for Egyptian paste is given below:

Feldspar	(parts by weight)	40
Flint		20
Kaolin		15
Ball clay		5
Sodium bicarbonate		6
Soda ash		6
Whiting		5
Fine white sand		8

This should be fired to cone 08 (950°C).

As mentioned earlier, potters today are less willing to accept the pot, as it comes out of the glaze firing, as a final statement. The desire to continue working on the piece can take many forms; for some it takes the form of adding further decoration or embellishments to the surface, usually in the form of painting and re-firing. The repeated firing of a pot can lead to cracking, bloating and the loss or reduction of previous decoration. To avoid this it is necessary to reduce the firing temperature at each stage. This can mean that materials and pigments must be selected that are suitable for that temperature range and the changing state of the ceramic. For some potters, formal qualities are given emphasis by the addition of other materials after the firing. These can be wires, cane, feathers, metal or wood additions that can emphasise spatial considerations or create greater awareness of the qualities of clay and glaze by using contrasting materials and additions.

Joining parts together after firing

The need to join fired elements together or add to the form after firing presents the potter with new problems. Quite often forms are too large to fit into the kiln and have to be made in sections and joined together after the firing, like those made by Sara Radstone.

Resin-based adhesives are very useful for this type of join and are available in several forms, but usually come as two part resin and hardener packs. Resin-based adhesives can also be used to join non-ceramic materials to clay.

Mechanical joins can be made using special bolts that have spring or gravity toggles that open or expand inside the cavity as the bolt is tightened. Jill Crowley has used this method to join her cat heads onto their box bases.

Today, with equipment such as sandblasters, grinders and polishers, it is possible to work on the fired clay itself. Although very different from the expressive use of plastic clay – clearly an important part of the handbuilding process – I feel this is really an extension of the process, rather than a completely different one.

Martin Smith is a ceramicist who has not been limited by the conventions of pottery making or its tradition and

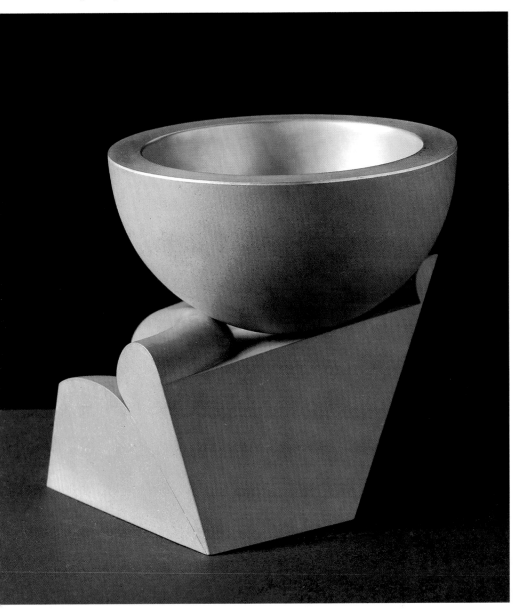

Left
Borromini Cloister Piece No. 2 by Martin Smith, 1981
Redware with aluminium

Below
Baroque Wall Piece No.1 by Martin Smith, 1981
Redware, black terra sigillata slip and slate

history. He does not feel confined by what is natural for the material or what is ethically correct, but approaches his work with a completely open attitude.

His pieces usually begin as very precise technical drawings, modified as they are realised as three dimensional forms. He has a particular interest in the

changing state of clay and how it can be worked at each stage. The initial shapes are often thrown or press moulded, but much of his work goes on before and after the manipulation of the clay, in the making of the moulds, templates and casting. After the firing he continues to work on the clay by sawing, grinding, routing and hand polishing with diamond pads. His uses a diamond saw and a lapidary wheel which is more appropriate for the clay when it has returned to its stonelike form rather than its mud or plastic state. This stage of the process has been compared to the cold working processes in glass making.

In his forms he explores ideas about the interior and exterior as well as demonstrating a concern for contrasts and opposites. He has added metal and stone components to contrast with the clay form and he often brings in a random element to contrast with the precision of the overall form. In his early vessels he used the unpredictable qualities of raku firings to contrast with the formality of the striped decoration and, in more recent work, he has incorporated sawdust or mineral perlite into the clay body, giving a random pitted texture to the surface once it has burned away. Parts of the pitted surface are then treated with a metal leaf that gives a shiny gold, platinum, aluminium or copper surface to contrast with the mattness of the remaining clay surfaces.

Martin Smith's approach to clay is a combination of art, design and technology that puts him on the edge of handbuilt ceramics.

Neil Brownsword is a potter who has been influenced by Martin Smith's cold working of the clay after it has been fired. His imaginative and at times surreal figures are assembled forms from previously fired ceramic pieces and also sometimes include other materials.

He uses slip-cast and press-moulded shapes or objects which are made and then fired and glazed separately. He sometimes combines these with fragments of pottery and other found objects. He works intuitively, sometimes allowing the glaze to join one piece to another, but usually he drills the pieces using a water cooled diamond-tipped drill to make the holes through which a metal armature is threaded to hold them in place. The shapes are filled with an epoxy filler (car repair filler) which not only holds them in place, but fixes them to the armature. Epoxy resin adhesive is used to join the forms together. Nails, screws and Nichrome wire are also used and these are often left exposed to contrast with the glossy low temperature, brightly coloured glazes.

There are artists who use handbuilt ceramic elements as central and important parts of their work, but do not see themselves as potters. One of these artists is **Paul Astbury** who prefers to call himself a sculptor rather than a potter. He has used small slabs of clay which are attached to a range of everyday objects, such as articles of clothing, cardboard boxes, car tyres and chairs. The slabs of clay are bolted onto the objects as a skin.

Similarly a small tree was wrapped in clay as cylinders of clay were threaded over the trunk, branches and twigs to become a 'Tree in a Landscape', where Paul Astbury saw the clay as representing the landscape.

In his more conceptual work he has used slip cast forms which have been

Left
Line and Displacement No. IV by Martin Smith, 1992
Redware with gold leaf

Left
He Only Wanted One Thing
by Neil Brownsword

Above
Don't Let The Little Head Rule The Big Head
by Neil Brownsword, 1996 h. 42 cm

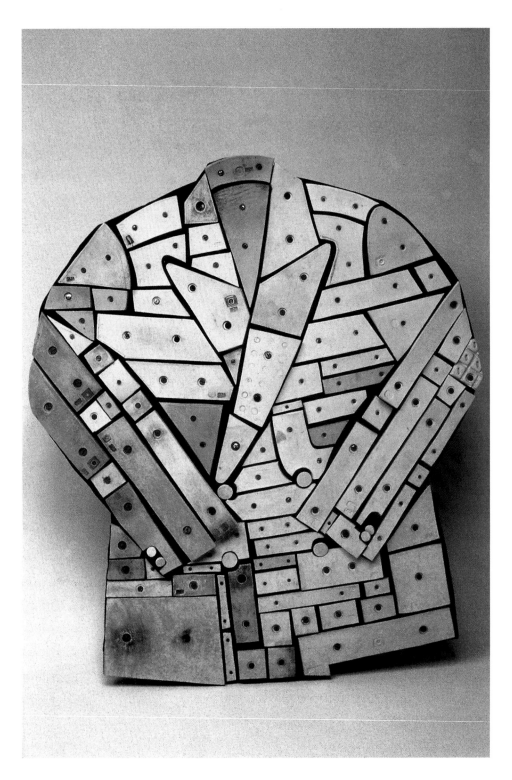

embedded in soft clay while still in their raw unfired state. These have then been encased in plastic vacuum-formed containers where they have been open to the effects of gravity and the continuous evaporation and condensation of the moisture inside the plastic container. The pieces were continuously changing and the transformation observed as the clay forms settled and disappeared or became crusty and mould covered.

Paul Astbury is not a potter in the traditional sense, but in his work as a conceptual artist he uses the techniques of the potter and explores the nature of clay in ways that blur boundaries and question definitions.

Matter of Life and Death by Paul Astbury, 1998
Clay, plastic wood and metal

Glossary of Terms

Alumina
An oxide of aluminium (Al_2O_3).
Supplied as calcined alumina or alumina hydrate.

Ball clay
Highly plastic refractory clay. Fine grained sedimentary clay.

Banding wheel or **'whirler'**
A revolving metal wheel head mounted on a pedestal base. It is turned by hand. to help in the decoration of a pot or to turn the pot or form around.

Bat
A board of wood, plaster or fired clay on which the work is placed.

Biscuit or **bisque**
Pottery which has been fired to an insoluble, but porous, state.

Body
A mixed or prepared clay that forms the structure of a pot.

Burnishing
Polishing with a stone or tool on leatherhard clay or slip to make a surface sheen.

Casting
Forming clay shapes by pouring slip into a porous mould.

Cheesehard
See leatherhard.

Cottle
The enclosing wall of clay, wood, plastic or linoleum built around the clay model or master to contain the plaster of Paris when it is poured.

Crystalline glazes
Large crystals grown on the glaze surface during firing and cooling, primarily induced by high zinc oxide and low alumina content in glazes.

Deflocculation
The addition of a catalyst or electrolyte to a clay and water slip to reduce the amount of water required while keeping the fluidity. Sodium silicate and sodium carbonate are usually used.

Earthenware
Pottery fired to as low as 800°C or as high as 1200°C.

Electrolyte
When used in connection with slip casting it is used as a deflocculant *(see deflocculant).*

Enamel
A low temperature glaze applied over another already fired glaze.

Greenware
Unfired clay ware.

Grog
Crushed fired pottery, varying in coarseness from fine dust to the texture of granulated sugar. Added to plastic clay it adds texture, mechanical strength, quickens drying and decreases shrinkage.

Kidney
A kidney shaped tool made of flexible steel for scraping or of stiff rubber for pressing and smoothing clay.

Leatherhard or **cheesehard**
Leatherhard clay is dry enough not to be soft and sticky but still soft enough to be worked.

Lute
To join leatherhard clay surfaces together with slip or slurry.

Natch
Usually small indentations and projections used as keys or means of locating and the registering of mould parts.

Plaster of Paris
A soft porous stone resulting from the combination of dehydrated gypsum and water.

Plastic
When applied to clay it means that the clay is soft enough to be shaped and capable of retaining its shape.

Porcelain
White stoneware, usually translucent when thin. Fired 1260°C and above.

Porosity
The amount of 'pore' space in the clay.

Press mould
A one or two piece mould into which plastic clay is pressed by hand or with a tool.

Primary clay
Clays that are found on the site where they were formed.

Raku
A low fired earthenware in which the pots are taken from the hot kiln and plunged into water, sometimes having been previously smoked in some combustible material like sawdust or straw to reduce the metal oxides and so give different colours.

Refractory
Resistant to heat, capable of standing high temperatures in the range of 1300°C and higher.

Sedimentary or **Secondary clays**
Primary clays that have been moved from their site of formation by natural forces.

Sgraffito
A technique whereby a layer of slip or glaze is scratched through to reveal the contrasting colour of the clay or body.

Slip
Clay in very liquid state. Suspension of clay in water.

Slurry
A rough mixture of clay and water.

Spare
The extra or 'spare' space at the top of the mould which acts as a pouring hole for the slip.

Stoneware
Pottery which has been fired to a hard and non vitrious state above 1200°C.

Surform
A serrated blade which is used to scrape down plaster moulds, and slab pots to make them smooth.

Template or Profile
A pattern or cutting guide used to shape or cut clay.

Undercut
Area on a model which prevents its removal or withdrawal from the mould.

Vitrify
The fusion or melting of a body during firing.

Wedging
The cutting and reforming of lumps of plastic clay preparatory to kneading to ensure an even texture.

Whirler
See banding wheel.

Bibliography

BILLINGTON, Dora, *The Technique of Pottery*, Batsford, London, 1966

BIRKS, Tony, *Art of the Modern Potter*, Country Life Books, London, 1976

BLANDINO, Betty, *Coiled Pottery Traditional and Contemporary Ways*, A & C Black, London, 1984

CAMERON, Elisabeth and LEWIS, Philippa, *Potters on Pottery*, Evans Brothers, London, 1976

CARDEW, Michael, *Pioneer Pottery*, Longman, 1969

CASSON, Michael, *The Craft of the Potter*, BBC Publications, 1977

CASSON, Michael, *Pottery in Britain Today*, Alec Tiranti, 1967

COOPER, Emmanuel, *A History of Pottery*, Longman, 1972

COWLEY, David, *Moulded and Slip Cast Pottery and Ceramics*, Batsford, London, 1984

DORMER, Peter, *The New Ceramics*, Thames and Hudson, London, 1995

HAMILTON, David, *Manual of Pottery and Ceramics*, Thames and Hudson, London, 1974

LANE, Peter, *Studio Ceramics*, William Collins, London, 1983

LANE, Peter, *Ceramic Form*, William Collins, 1988

LEACH, Bernard, *A Potters Book*, Souvenir Press, 1976

PETERSON, Susan, *Working with Clay*, Laurence King, 1998

RAWSON, Philip, *Ceramics*, Oxford University Press, 1971

RHODES, Daniel, *Clay and Glazes*, Chilton, Philadelphia, 1995

RICE, Paul and GOWING Christopher, *British Studio Ceramics in the Twentieth Century*, Barry and Jenkins, 1989

ROGERS, Mary, *Pottery and Porcelain, A Handbuilders Approach*, Alphabooks, Sherbourne, 1979 (now Collins, London and Watson Guptill, New York)

ROSE, Muriel, *Artist Potters in England*, Faber and Faber, 1955

TRIPLETT, Kathy, *Handbuilt Ceramics*, Lark Books, 1997

WALLER, Jane, *Hand-built Ceramics*, Batsford, London, 1996

WOODY, Elsbeth, *Handbuilding/Ceramic Forms*, John Murray, 1979

The Raw and the Cooked: New Work in Clay in Britain, Museum of Modern Art, Oxford, 1993

Suppliers

UK Suppliers
Alec Tiranti, 27 Warren Street, London W1P 5DG
Bath Potters' Supplies, 2 Dorset Close, Bath, Avon BA2 3RF
Brick House Ceramic Supplies, Cock Green, Felstead, Essex, CM6 3JE
Potclays Ltd, Brick Kiln Lane, Etruria, Stoke on Trent, Staffs. ST4 7BP
Potterycrafts Ltd, Campbell Road, Stoke on Trent, Staffs. ST4 4ET

North American Suppliers
American Art Clay Company 4717, W. 16th Street, Indianapolis IN 46222
A.R.T. Studio Clay Company, 1555 Louis Avenue, Elk Grove Village Il 60007
Axner Pottery Supply, P.O. Box1484, Oviedo, Florida 32765
Davens, 198 Murray Drive, Atlanta, Ga 30341
Duncan Ceramics Products Inc., PO Box 7827, Fresno, California 93727
General Suppliers, Continental Clay Company, 1101 Stinson Blvd, N.E.,
    Minneapolis MN 55413
Laguna Clay Company, 14400 Lomitas Avenue, City of Industry, CA 91746
Mile High Ceramics, 77 Lipan, Denver, Colorado 80223-1580
Minnesota Clay Co., 8001 Grand Avenue South, Bloomington MN 55420
The Potter's Shop, 31 Thorpe Road, Needham, Massachusettes, MA 02194
Tucker's Pottery Supplies Inc.,15 West Pearce Street, Unit 7, Richmond Hill,
    Ontario, L4B 1H6

Australian Suppliers
Claycraft Supplies Pty. Ltd., 29 O'Connell Terrace, Bowens Hills, Queensland 4006
Claymates Pottery Supplies, 120 Parker Street, Maroochydare, Queensland 4558
Jackson Ceramic Craft, 94 Jersey Street, Jolimont, Western Australia 6014
Keane Ceramics Pty Ltd., RMD 3971 Debenham Road, Somersby NSW 2250
Potters Equipment, 13/42 New Street, Ringwood, Victoria 3134

New Zealand Suppliers
Coastal Ceramics, 124 Rimu Road, Paraparaumu, 84377 Pram

Index

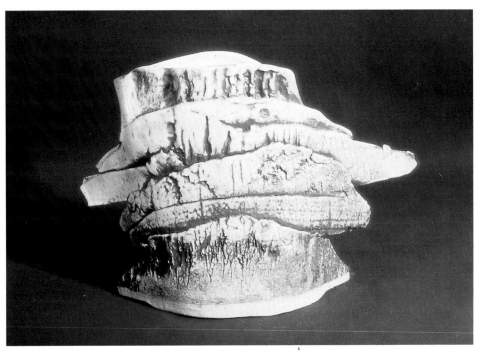

Landscape Form 1997 by Michael Hardy. h 20 cm w 30 cm.